A Lucan Reader

B̸c **LATIN** Readers
Series Editor:
Ronnie Ancona

These readers, written by experts in the field, provide well annotated Latin selections to be used as authoritative introductions to Latin authors, genres, or topics, for intermediate or advanced college Latin study. Their relatively small size (covering 500–600 lines) makes them ideal to use in combination. Each volume includes a comprehensive introduction, bibliography for further reading, Latin text with notes at the back, and complete vocabulary. Sixteen volumes are scheduled for publication; others are under consideration. Check our website for updates: www.BOLCHAZY.com.

A Lucan Reader
Selections from *Civil War*

Susanna Braund

Bolchazy-Carducci Publishers, Inc.
Mundelein, Illinois USA

Series Editor: Ronnie Ancona
Volume Editor: Laurie Haight Keenan
Contributing Editor: Timothy Beck
Cover Design & Typography: Adam Phillip Velez
Map: Mapping Specialists, Ltd.

A Lucan Reader
Selections from Civil War

Susanna Braund

Bolchazy-Carducci Publishers, Inc.
1570 Baskin Road
Mundelein, Illinois 60060
www.bolchazy.com

Printed in the United States of America
2009
by United Graphics

ISBN 978-0-86516-661-5

Library of Congress Cataloging-in-Publication Data

Lucan, 39-65.
  [Pharsalia. Selections]
  A Lucan reader : selections from Civil war / Susanna Braund.
      p. cm. -- (Latin reader series)
  Text in Latin; introduction, notes, and commentary in English.
  ISBN 978-0-86516-661-5 (pbk. : alk. paper) 1. Rome--History--Civil War, 49-45 B.C.--
Poetry. 2. Latin language--Readers--Poetry. I. Braund, Susanna Morton. II. Title.

  PA6478.A2 2008
  873'.01--dc22

                                                            2008040485

Contents

Preface

I am delighted to have been offered the opportunity to share my passion for the poetry of Lucan by Bolchazy-Carducci Publishers. Lucan is not often read by students at the advanced level and almost never at the intermediate level. There are reasons for this, apart from fashion. His Latin can be very difficult and the articulation of his ideas sometimes seems downright perverse. But whether his Latin is really more difficult than any other author of the post-Augustan period is debatable. And to understand how and why he narrates— or refuses to narrate—the story of the civil war between Caesar and Pompey is to gain an important insight into early imperial poetry. It is my fervent hope that the brief selection from Lucan's *Civil War* offered in this volume will provoke students to study this amazing poem in greater depth.

I here express my gratitude to Ronnie Ancona for supporting my unexpected proposal to produce a volume on Lucan and for her ongoing help during production. Laurie Haight Keenan at the Press has also been most helpful. Elaine Fantham, Vincent Hunink, Corby Kelly, and Toph Marshall have all assisted in different ways. Two dear friends have made special contributions. Victoria Pagán, whose understanding of imperial literature and of the needs of teachers and students alike is unparalleled, read the whole manuscript at very short notice and made suggestions large and small that improved the book significantly. My largest debt of gratitude is to Jo Wallace-Hadrill for producing the total vocabulary—a task requiring, and receiving, the most painstaking attention to detail. Without Jo's contribution the sheer joy of writing this book might have been overwhelmed by the challenge of generating the vocabulary list. I knew I needed to find a special person for this role and I count myself fortunate that Jo was happy to undertake it.

It is my final pleasure to dedicate this book to John Henderson, with whom I first read Lucan, to the memory of Charles Tesoriero, who was a fellow enthusiast for Lucan's Erichtho, and to all my students, past, present, and future.

SUSANNA BRAUND
Bowen Island, British Columbia

Introduction

◌ Lucan's life and times

Lucan is an intriguing figure. He moved in court circles from a young age and was a prolific poet. He seems to have enjoyed the favor of the emperor Nero, two years his elder, for a while, but was later in effect silenced. Finally he joined a conspiracy to overthrow Nero but was compelled to commit suicide at the age of 25.

Marcus Annaeus Lucanus was born in 39 CE at Corduba (modern Córdova), Spain, into a wealthy and prominent family. The rhetorician and historian Seneca the Elder was his grandfather and the Stoic philosopher Seneca the Younger, later tutor to the young Nero, was his father's brother. Lucan was raised at Rome and received an education typical for the sons of the elite, consisting of the study of literature and rhetoric (public speaking). He may also have studied Stoic philosophy with a freedman of Seneca. Nero invited him into his circle of close friends and gave him prominence in Roman public life with the bestowal of the positions of quaestor and augur, even though Lucan was below the minimum age for the quaestorship. Lucan reciprocated with a eulogy of the emperor that he recited at the Neronia, the quinquennial games established by Nero in 60 CE. But in 64 CE Nero banned Lucan from public recitation of his poetry and from practicing advocacy in the law-courts, thus in effect removing him from the public eye. We do not know the reason for this rift. Our sources personalize the matter with stories of Nero's jealousy of Lucan's manifest literary abilities. But there may have been political reasons for Nero's action, perhaps connected with Seneca's enforced retirement from public life in 62 CE. In any case, early in 65 CE Lucan joined the so-called "Pisonian conspiracy" that planned to replace Nero with Calpurnius Piso; the biographer Suetonius describes Lucan as the "standard-bearer" of the conspirators. But the plot was exposed and the leading players were either executed or forced to commit suicide. Lucan chose to commit suicide in April 65 CE, a fate shared by the end of 66 CE by his father and uncle too. The account of Lucan's suicide provided by the historian Tacitus (*Annals* 15.70) has him reciting some lines from one of his own poems as his last words.

The accession of Nero in 54 CE was celebrated by many as a new golden age, redolent of the reign of Augustus, and literature appears to have been revitalized under the patronage and encouragement of the emperor, who had artistic interests and literary ambitions himself. According to our sources, Lucan contributed to this flowering of poetry with prolific productivity. Although his epic poem on the civil war between Caesar and Pompey is the only poem of his to survive, we have fragments of his *Journey to the Underworld, Tale of Troy, Orpheus*, and epigrams, and we know by title alone of his *Eulogy of Nero, Address to Polla* (his wife), ten books of occasional poetry, *Saturnalia, Medea* (a tragedy), fourteen books of pantomime libretti, a poem *On the Burning of Rome*, and *Letters from Campania* (probably in verse) as well as prose orations.

It seems reasonable to regard his epic poem, *Civil War*, as his major achievement. The poem has generated controversy and scholarly dispute concerning its title and its political position. Many scholars have called it *Pharsalia*, on the basis of some lines from Book 9 where Lucan links Caesar's immortality with his own (980–86). He promises to Caesar that "future ages will read me and you" and that "our Pharsalia shall live" for ever.

But it seems clear that he here refers to the battle of Pharsalia as won by Caesar and as recorded by Lucan in his poem. Certainly, no surviving manuscript gives *Pharsalia* as the title, while the majority of manuscripts have *De bello ciuili*, "On the Civil War." Some scholars prefer to use the title *Bellum Ciuile*, simply "Civil War." It is even imaginable to think of the opening line of the poem as its title, *Bella . . . plus quam ciuilia*, "wars worse [literally, "more"] than civil wars," given that many poems in antiquity were known by their opening words.

Lucan's political position in relation to Nero and the Principate is just as intractable. Some scholars have pointed to Lucan's participation in an attempted political coup against Nero (the "Pisonian conspiracy") and have retrojected Lucan's hostility towards Nero. On this view, Lucan's flattery of Nero at the opening of the poem must be heavily ironic (see 1.33–45 in this volume) and marked by doublespeak. This interpretation is fueled by the discomfort that modern western culture experiences when confronted with extravagant panegyric. However, many other societies have generated praise addressed to rulers that is similarly effusive, or even more effusive—the English and French courts in the seventeenth and eighteenth centuries, for example, or some modern Arab monarchies. It is certainly possible to take Lucan's praise of Nero as the expected tribute by a poet to the autocrat who held absolute power in the Roman state. There are certainly plenty of analogues from within Roman culture—the praise offered to Octavian (not yet Augustus) by Virgil in his *Georgics* and to Augustus by Horace in his *Odes* (although some critics are as skeptical of the message there as they are of Lucan's attitude here) as well as the eulogies to later emperors composed by poets such as Statius and Martial.

Some have read Lucan as a "Republican" because of his participation in the Pisonian conspiracy and because of his condemnation of Caesar, who inaugurated one-man rule at Rome when he assumed the dictatorship in the early 40s BCE. Although this view of "Lucan the Republican" is understandable at the zenith of his popularity in the anti-monarchical and revolutionary climates of seventeenth century England and eighteenth century France, it involves a profound misunderstanding of Roman politics in the first century CE. The Principate was a fact by the time that Lucan was writing and it is clear that the aim of the conspirators was not to restore the Republic but to replace Nero with another emperor who would treat the Roman elite with more dignity and respect.

To read Lucan's hostility towards Caesar as a manifestation of Republican or even anti-Neronian sentiment is also too simplistic. Although Nero was certainly a "Julian" emperor in his descent from

Augustus and through him from Julius Caesar, Augustus' great-uncle and adoptive father, he may not have identified closely with Julius Caesar. Rather, it is possible that he identified with the Pompeian party through his (blood) ancestor Lucius Domitius Ahenobarbus, who is picked out for favorable treatment by Lucan. Domitius, who was Nero's great-great-grandfather, appears twice in the poem, in Book 2 when he displays a noble bearing on his surrender to Caesar and in Book 7 when his death receives possibly the most heroic treatment of any in the poem. Since other accounts depict Domitius' behavior in much less favorable terms, it is clear that Lucan sought to present Nero's ancestor positively. In short, to my mind there is no reason to posit any growing discontent with either Nero or the Principate. Rather, Lucan seems to have flourished under Nero until late in 64 or early in 65 CE when he decided to join the conspiracy; we can never know whether his reason was simply Nero's ban or broader political issues. The issue of Lucan's ideological stance remains the most contentious issue in the interpretation of his poem. The clearest account of the problem is still that of Frederick Ahl in *Lucan: An Introduction* (Ithaca and London, 1976) 35–61.

Lucan chose as his topic for his epic poem the civil war between Caesar and Pompey. Below I shall outline the events of the civil war, discuss Lucan's choice of genre, give an outline of the poem, analyze its scope and structure, and discuss its literary dimensions, including Lucan's relationship with his predecessors in the genre, particularly Virgil. Topics include Lucan's handling of the gods and the supernatural, the marked Stoic dimension of the poem, the three protagonists and the other characters, the strategies he adopts to maximize the horror of his subject-matter and, finally, the characteristics of his Latin. After a protracted lack for appreciation of Lucan's achievement and years of scholarly neglect, happily there is now an abundance of excellent scholarship to enhance our reading of Lucan. I have selected a few items for the bibliography, which appears at the end of the Introduction.

↶ *The civil war between Caesar and Pompey*

Lucan chose to compose his epic poem about events from relatively recent history—the civil war between Caesar and Pompey that started when Caesar crossed the Rubicon in 49 BCE. The civil war set in motion a sequence of events that led to the supremacy of Octavian, Julius Caesar's heir and adoptive son, who had himself proclaimed Augustus in 27 BCE. Augustus is usually regarded as the first emperor, or *princeps*, and he made every attempt to keep the succession within his family. At his death in 14 CE he was succeeded by his stepson, Tiberius, who ruled until 37 CE. He in turn was succeeded by Gaius, whose nickname was Caligula, the son of Germanicus, Tiberius' nephew and adoptive son. Gaius ruled for just four years before he was murdered and replaced by his uncle Claudius, who ruled 41–54 CE, until he was allegedly poisoned by his wife Agrippina in her machinations to make her son Nero emperor. With Nero's death in 68 CE, the so-called Julio-Claudian dynasty came to an end.

The civil war of 49–45 BCE can only be understood through events that led up to it—as Lucan himself understands very well, supplying a lengthy consideration of its causes at the beginning of Book 1 of his poem. Analysis of the background events usually begins in 60 BCE, following Sir Ronald Syme, the great Roman historian, in his crucial book, *The Roman Revolution*, first published in 1939 and still in print. The year 60 BCE saw an informal coalition, often called the "First Triumvirate," between Julius Caesar, just returned from a successful campaign in Spain, with the millionaire Marcus Crassus and the brilliant general Gnaeus Pompeius, Pompey the Great, who had recently returned from his conquest and political reorganization of the Near East. The collaboration was sealed by the marriage of Caesar's daughter Julia to Pompey the next year and as consul in 59 BCE Caesar was able to ratify the coalition's legislation as well as set up a five-year command in Gaul for himself. The command was not only a vehicle for his military ambitions, both in terms of the glory that came from conquest and the power that came from the loyalty of troops bound more to their individual commander rather than to the Roman state. It also brought him immunity from prosecution, which was a major concern for any Roman who had held high office. In Roman Republican political life, it was absolutely normal for political enemies to take their revenge via prosecution, but this could happen only once the individual had returned to private status. Since anyone who rose to the highest positions had inevitably made many enemies on the way, the fear of prosecution was very real.

The coalition weathered some bumpy moments to be consolidated in 56 BCE at a meeting at Luca (modern Lucca) with the violent installation of Pompey and Crassus as consuls for the next year. The consuls used their position to protect themselves with five-year commands in Spain and Syria respectively and extended Caesar's command of Gaul into the year 50 BCE, a measure designed to give him uninterrupted power until it was legal for him to stand for the consulship again. But the coalition did not last that long.

In 54 BCE the bond between Caesar and Pompey was weakened by the death of Julia in childbirth and in 53 BCE Crassus was killed by the Parthians at the battle of Carrhae. In 52 BCE, after months of anarchy, Pompey became sole consul, a constitutionally unprecedented position. He used his power to enact measures, some of which appeared to support Caesar's position but others of which clearly undermined it. His shift away from Caesar and back towards what we might call the senatorial party was marked by his marriage to Cornelia, daughter of one of the traditionalists.

Caesar had nearly been out-maneuvered by Pompey, but not quite. In 50 BCE he persuaded Curio, one of the tribunes, to veto the legislation that would jeopardize his position, by paying off Curio's massive debts. As the year progressed, civil war seemed more and more inevitable. When in December Curio proposed the motion to the Senate that both Pompey and Caesar should give up their provinces and armies, support was overwhelming. However, the consul Marcellus dismissed the Senate without implementing the motion and a few days later, in response to a rumor that Caesar was invading Italy, entrusted the defense of Italy to Pompey. In the first few days of 49 BCE, the new consul Lentulus overrode the veto of the new tribunes

Antony and Cassius who were now acting for Caesar, had the Senate declare a state of emergency, and started the process of replacing Caesar as governor of Gaul. This gave Caesar the pretext he needed to act: he could claim that he was defending the tribunes and their rights.

So in January 49 BCE Caesar crossed the Rubicon, which was the boundary between his province of Cisalpine Gaul and Italy. In response to his rapid advance down the east coast of Italy, Pompey and the Senate withdrew from Rome to Brundisium and in March sailed across to Epirus, leaving Italy in Caesar's control (Books 1–2). Caesar entered Rome, seized the Treasury, and then went to Massilia where he began to besiege the city (Book 3) and moved on to Spain, where he defeated Pompey's generals (Book 4). Meanwhile in Africa his lieutenant Curio was defeated and killed by King Juba, an ally of Pompey (Book 4). Caesar returned to Rome in December to be elected consul and in January crossed to Epirus (Book 5) and faced Pompey at Dyrrachium (Book 6). Pompey then moved east to Thessaly and the two armies met in the battle of Pharsalia on 9 August 48 BCE, where Caesar inflicted a resounding defeat on Pompey (Book 7). Pompey fled with the remnants of the Senate (other senators went directly to Africa with Cato and Pompey's son Gnaeus) and was killed on his arrival in Egypt on 29 September (Book 8). Caesar arrived in Alexandria three days later (Books 9–10), waged war against Ptolemy XIII and in the spring of 47 BCE established Cleopatra as ruler. In the summer he returned to Rome, but in December crossed over to Africa to deal with the Pompeian forces that had mustered there under Pompey's father-in-law Scipio. Caesar finally took Thapsus after besieging it for four months. Soon afterwards, Cato the Younger, one of the Pompeian leaders, committed suicide at Utica. As a result of his victory Caesar was voted dictator for ten years and he returned to Rome to celebrate a fourfold triumph. But the war was not yet over. Before the end of 46 BCE he had to go to Spain to face the troops that Pompey's sons had assembled there. Caesar ended the brief campaign with his victory at the battle of Munda on 17 March 45 BCE. Caesar then returned to Rome where he remained until his assassination in March 44 BCE.

Our sources for the events of the civil war include Caesar's own commentaries on the *Civil War* (three books) as well as accounts written by his officers, the *Alexandrian War* covering 48–47 BCE, the *African War* on the events of 47–46 BCE, and the *Spanish War* on the campaign that climaxed with the battle of Munda; the narratives written in Greek by Appian in the second century CE (*Civil Wars* Book 2) and by Dio Cassius in the early third century CE (*Roman History* Books 41–43); and the relevant *Lives* by Plutarch (also in Greek, written in the late first and early second century CE), most obviously those of Pompey, Caesar, and Cato the Younger. The sources available to Lucan included Caesar's account and the narrative written by Livy as part of his monumental history of Rome, *From the Foundation of Rome*; unfortunately, these books of Livy do not survive. Since Lucan could assume his audience's familiarity with the events of the civil war, and since his choice of genre was epic poetry not prose historiography, he did not feel any need to provide relentless detail. In fact, he at times omits, minimizes, amplifies, and even invents incidents and minor characters. A good example of this is the appearance of Cicero in Pompey's camp at the battle of Pharsalia (Book 7): we know from Plutarch that Cicero was not present, but dramatically it makes good sense to deploy him as the spokesman of the Senate. Another example is Lucan's account of the assassination of Pompey in Book 8, where a comparison with the cluttered but probably more reliable account by Plutarch demonstrates clearly Lucan's tendency towards simplification for dramatic effect.

❧ *Lucan's choice of genre*

Lucan chose to write an epic poem in the long-established hexameter meter. This decision sets some parameters for our judgment of his achievement. He is not inviting comparison with the writers of historiographical narrative. Rather, his models are his predecessors in the epic genre, above all, Virgil, whose *Aeneid* was an instant success when the emperor Augustus published it after Virgil's death in 19 BCE. In fact, the poem was so esteemed that it immediately became a set-text for Roman schoolboys and a text against which any subsequent epic poet was forced to measure himself. Virgil's achievement in the *Aeneid* is often regarded as the high point of Latin literature, after which there could only be decline. That attitude explains the labels "Golden" and "Silver" that have been applied to Augustan and post-Augustan literature respectively. But instead of constructing an acme and subsequent decline, it is more valuable to consider how the preeminence of the *Aeneid* inspired subsequent poets to define themselves and their projects differently—a topic explored brilliantly by Philip Hardie in his book *The Epic Successors of Virgil* (Cambridge, 1993). As I proceed to indicate some of the characteristics of Lucan's poetry, including manifestations of his deliberate differences from Virgil, I intend to make the case for reading Lucan on his own terms and for valuing his achievement as one of the most original poets produced by Rome.

∾ *Epic and the theme of civil war*

When we think of Greco-Roman epic poems, Greek mythological epics such as the *Iliad* and *Odyssey* and *Argonautica* immediately come to mind. In Latin literature, Virgil's *Aeneid* too arguably belongs in that category, in that it deals with events in the distant past before the foundation of Rome, although Virgil forges strong links between past and present. Against that backdrop, Lucan's decision to tackle the relatively recent civil war looks like an innovation. But there was a strong tradition of historical epic at Rome, starting with the earliest Latin epics, Naevius' *Punic War* (written in the Saturnian meter) and Ennius' *Annals* (written, like the Homeric epics, in the dactylic hexameter), composed in the late third century BCE and second century BCE respectively. The fragments of poems on the civil wars written under the emperor Augustus and during the first century CE that survive demonstrate that historical epic was still alive and that the topic was considered viable. More than that, such poems seem to have been comfortable depicting the involvement of the gods in the action. It turns out that one of Lucan's chief innovations was not his choice of recent history but his dispensing with the expected divine machinery (as Denis Feeney shows in Chapter 6 of *The Gods in Epic* [Oxford, 1991]).

∾ *Outline of the poem, contextualizing the excerpts in this volume*

Lucan starts by stating the theme of his poem, the civil war between Caesar and Pompey, expressing his regret about Rome's embroilment in civil war, but declaring that everything was worthwhile to have Nero as emperor (**1.1–45**). After asking Nero to inspire his poetry, he analyzes various causes of the civil war: the inevitable collapse of mighty structures, the impossibility of sharing power at Rome, the death of Crassus, and the death of Julia (Caesar's daughter and Pompey's wife). He devotes most attention to the personalities of the two leaders, introducing similes in which Pompey is compared to a massive old oak tree and Caesar is compared to a lightning-bolt (**1.67–157**). After a brief tirade against Rome's luxury and immorality, Lucan finally begins his narrative of the civil war. Caesar advances to the Rubicon and after being halted for a moment by a vision of Rome personified, crosses into Italy (**1.183–228**). He advances through Italy and is joined by his supporter Curio, the previous year's tribune, now fleeing from Rome in fear for his life. After scenes depicting Caesar as a commander and a catalogue of his troops, a standard feature of epic, Lucan portrays the panic at Rome at the (false) reports of Caesar's imminent invasion (**1.486–504**). The rest of Book 1 is devoted to the supernatural: terrible prodigies and portents, an unsuccessful purification of the city and prophecies of doom, an astrologer's prediction of civil war, and finally a prophecy of the events of the civil war delivered by a Roman matron in a frenzy.

Book 2 commences with an old man's lengthy recollections of the previous civil wars, between Marius and Sulla, and then introduces the grim Stoic moralist Cato the Younger, the third protagonist in the poem, who will take over as leader after Pompey's death. Cato is depicted first in conversation with Brutus, the future assassin of Caesar, and then renewing his marriage-vows with Marcia in a simple, rather bleak ceremony designed to show his austerity. Lucan then narrates Pompey's withdrawal from Rome to Campania and Caesar's unstoppable advance through Italy, including the surrender of Corfinium and with it Pompey's general Domitius Ahenobarbus (an ancestor of Nero), who is spared by Caesar. Unable to inspire his troops, Pompey withdraws to Brundisium, pursued by Caesar, who tries to blockade him. Pompey's fleet manages to escape and Caesar is welcomed into the city.

Book 3 starts with Pompey's voyage to Epirus, during which his dead wife Julia appears to him as a Fury and vows to hound him forever (3.8–35). Back in Italy, Caesar marches to Rome and ransacks the Treasury. After a catalogue of Pompey's troops, Lucan shifts the focus to Massilia in Gaul for the rest of the book. Refused access to Massilia, Caesar begins a siege, cutting down a sacred grove in the process (3.399–445). Then his troops attack the city from the sea and Lucan delivers his first battle narrative: his sea-battle is a display of his interest in violent and strange deaths.

The setting of Book 4 is Spain, Illyria, and Africa. In Spain, Caesar takes on Pompey's generals near the town of Ilerda. After Caesar experiences flood and famine and the Pompeians thirst and after an incident of fraternization that ends in a massacre, the Pompeian troops surrender. In Illyria on the Adriatic shore Pompeian troops are besieging Caesar's general Antonius. The Caesarian troops attempt to escape on rafts, but one raft is trapped and those on board commit mutual suicide (i.e., they make a pact to kill one another) rather than be captured. Caesar's lieutenant Curio arrives in Africa, where he is told the story by a local of the fight between Hercules and Antaeus. He defeats the Pompeian commander but is himself defeated and killed by Pompey's ally King Juba.

Much of Book 5 is occupied by incidents that do not advance the narrative. First Lucan devotes a long passage to the consultation of the Delphic oracle in Greece by Appius, one of the Pompeian leaders. Then Caesar quells a mutiny among his troops. After going to Rome to be invested as dictator, he crosses with his troops across the Adriatic from Brundisium to Epirus, even though it is past the sailing season. Once he has arrived there and camped at Dyrrachium, he sends for his remaining forces in Italy to join him; because they delay, he attempts to cross back to Italy in a small boat. Lucan devotes the rest of the book to a narrative of the storm at sea that Lucan presents as a contest in which Caesar defiantly challenges the gods to overwhelm him. He does not make the crossing but he survives the elements and returns safely to his troops in Epirus. Book 5 ends with a touching episode in which Pompey decides to send his beloved wife Cornelia to the island of Lesbos for safety.

Book 6 starts with conflict between Caesar and Pompey: Pompey seizes Dyrrachium but is besieged by Caesar. As it attempts to break through Caesar's rampart, Pompey's army is driven back by the heroic efforts of one man, Scaeva. This is Lucan's version of another standard element in epic (like the catalogue in Book 1), the *aristeia*, or celebration of the "best exploits" of a single warrior. Eventually Pompey breaks out and Caesar heads for Thessaly, with Pompey in pursuit. The rest of the book is devoted to Thessaly, starting with an extended geographical description, displaying Lucan's learning and rhetorical skill. The night before battle Pompey's son Sextus consults the terrifying witch Erichtho about the outcome. Lucan provides a brilliantly atmospheric narrative of Erichtho's necromancy (literally "corpse-divination"), in which she selects a corpse to revive so that it can deliver a prophecy (**6.624–53**). The focus is on Erichtho's terrifying magic rites and her power to command the forces of the Underworld and not on the prophecy, which is vague.

Book 7 is devoted to the battle of Pharsalia. It starts with Pompey's dream and with his troops demanding battle. Against his better judgment, he concedes. An account of portents heightens the tension. Caesar delivers an inspiring speech to his men, in contrast with Pompey, whose battle-speech ends with a picture of defeat. Lucan then reflects on the devastating effect of the battle on his own times, again heightening tension. Once the battle begins, Lucan punctuates his narrative with authorial interventions expressing horror. He focuses on very few individuals—only Brutus (Lucan urges him to wait to kill Caesar) and Domitius, the ancestor of Nero who featured in Book 2 and whose death receives elaborated treatment here. Lucan expresses the difficulty of narrating individual deaths in civil warfare (**7.617–37**) and then narrates Pompey's dignified departure from the battlefield (**7.647–82**). Caesar captures Pompey's camp (**7.728–46**), but his troops have nightmares when they lie down to sleep, with

Caesar experiencing everyone else's nightmares and more. But the next morning he takes breakfast on the battlefield and commands that the dead be left unburied, for which Lucan remonstrates with him (7.760–811). After a grisly description of the birds and beasts devouring the corpses, Lucan addresses Thessaly, imagining future finds of relics of the battle.

The focus of Book 8 is Pompey and his death. First he flees fearfully and is reunited with Cornelia in a scene that moves everyone, including Pompey, to tears. As Pompey sails away, he sends his ally King Deiotarus to seek assistance from the Parthians, who were Rome's arch-enemies: this probably fictitious episode shows Pompey's lapse in judgment. In a meeting of the Senate in exile, Pompey urges that they take refuge in Parthia, but his proposal is defeated by a more powerful speech advocating refuge in Egypt with Ptolemy. Pompey bows to this and sets sail for Egypt. At the Egyptian court, the eunuch Pothinus successfully makes the case for the assassination of Pompey and a task force is dispatched to meet him. This moves Lucan to express his outrage at Ptolemy's intervention in Rome's civil war. His narrative of Pompey's murder brings out Pompey's thoughts of dying honorably along with Cornelia's desperate devotion to her husband (8.542–636). Lucan expresses horror that Pompey's head is cut off and embalmed (8.663–88). Book 8 concludes with the humble burial of Pompey's body by a loyal follower on the shore and Lucan's curse of Egypt.

Book 9 opens with the apotheosis of Pompey. Cato, who is the main character of the book, then assumes command and takes Pompey's forces to Africa. Once Cornelia has joined him there, Cato delivers a funeral oration for Pompey (9.190–217). The troops mutiny, declaring their devotion to Pompey alone, but Cato shames them into staying the course. He sets sail to King Juba, losing some of his ships in another storm at sea. Lucan takes the opportunity to include geographical and mythological material relevant to Africa. Cato leads his troops across land through the hazards of Libya— heat, wind, and thirst—to the temple of Jupiter Ammon where he declines to consult the oracle because of his Stoic outlook. Lucan now devotes more than three hundred lines to a narrative of the

snakes that afflict Cato's army and the cure offered by the local peo-
ple. Book 9 closes with the episode of Caesar's visit to the decayed
site of Troy, during which Lucan promises immortality to Caesar
(9.961–99), before he travels on to Egypt where he is presented with
Pompey's head and weeps feigned tears.

The incomplete Book 10 starts with Caesar's visit to the tomb
of Alexander the Great and Lucan's invective against Alexander.
When Ptolemy and Cleopatra vie for Caesar's favor, it is Cleopatra
who succeeds. She invites Caesar to a luxurious banquet that is de-
scribed lavishly by Lucan. During the banquet Caesar hears theories
about the source of the Nile. Meanwhile the eunuch Pothinus plots
to seize power by assassinating Caesar and Cleopatra; his task force
surrounds the palace. Caesar barricades himself in, but manages to
resist the onslaught. At this moment of extreme danger, Caesar is
inspired by the thought of his soldier Scaeva, who single-handedly
resisted the Pompeian army in Book 6. At this point, our text breaks
off, curiously at the same point as Caesar's narrative of the civil war
in his commentaries.

∾ *The scope and structure of the poem*

The poem breaks off partway through Book 10. Was it unfinished
at the time of Lucan's death in 65 CE or was part of the text lost at
a very early stage? Speculation about this and about the scope and
structure of the poem has produced very different interpretations.
Possible end-points proposed include the suicide of Cato after the
battle of Thapsus in 46 BCE, the assassination of Caesar in 44 BCE,
the battle of Philippi in 42 BCE, and the battle of Actium in 31 BCE.
Given that in ten books Lucan has covered the events of just twenty
months, Cato's suicide offers the most plausible solution and would
have been viable in an epic of twelve or sixteen books; the other theo-
ries require a much longer poem. This solution has the advantage of
literary coherence: Cato is introduced in the extant text as the third
protagonist; after Pompey's death, he is immediately depicted as the
leader of the senatorial faction; and his Stoicism and suicide would
have reprised prominent themes in the poem.

It is clear that the consultation of the witch Erichtho in Book 6 is designed as an inversion, or perversion, of Aeneas' visit to the Sibyl in Book 6 of Virgil's *Aeneid*. That suggests that Lucan may have planned a poem in twelve books as a challenge to the supreme position occupied by the *Aeneid*. At the same time, once we note that other post-Virgilian epics reject the twelve-book model—for example, Ovid's *Metamorphoses* in fifteen books and (after Lucan) Silius' *Punic Wars* in seventeen books—it becomes less necessary to postulate a twelve-book poem. In any case, Lucan's method of composition is more episodic than Virgil's and more closely resembles the structure of Ovid's epic poem. Given the importance of virtuosic rhetorical display in the early empire, it is easy to imagine the performance of excerpts in Nero's court—such as the entire necromancy episode that concludes Book 6 or Caesar's visit to Troy from Book 9.

✎ *The role of the gods, Fate, and Fortune*

Earlier epic deploys anthropomorphized deities as main movers of plot—just think of the interventions by Juno and Venus in Virgil's *Aeneid*, or the involvement in human life by the gods who appear in Ovid's *Metamorphoses*. Lucan's decision to abandon the traditional divine machinery is, then, very marked. And it was not for shortage of possibilities. He could easily have made Venus Caesar's champion, since she was claimed as his ancestor through Aeneas, and Hercules the supporter of the Pompeians; we are told that the passwords at the battle of Pharsalia were "Venus Victorious" (*Venus Victrix*) and "Hercules Unconquered" (*Hercules Inuictus*) respectively. Instead, we find only vague references to "the gods." He replaces the divine apparatus with the Stoic concepts of Fate and Fortune. The Stoics regarded Fate (*fatum* or *fata*) as destiny, as the fixed, immutable order of the world. Fortune they regarded as a fickle and capricious power capable of elevating or destroying any individual. On a Stoic reading of Lucan's poem, it was a fact and an act of Fate that Caesar was victorious and that Nero consequently became emperor (1.33), but it was Fortune who presided over Caesar's rise (e.g., 1.225–27) and Pompey's fall (e.g., 7.665–68). One important consequence of removing the traditional interventions of anthropomorphic divinities is that Lucan emphasizes the element of human responsibility for the horrors of civil warfare. There are no excuses for the atrocities performed. The concept of Fate makes the outcome terrifyingly inexorable and the concept of Fortune highlights the randomness of victimhood. These are deliberate choices by Lucan designed to increase the horror quotient of his poem.

✌ *The influence of Stoic ideas*

Lucan's deployment of Fate and Fortune is one aspect among many of the Stoic coloring of the poem. Lucan moved in Stoic circles—for example, his uncle Seneca, who was tutor to the young Nero, was committed to Stoicism and produced a prodigious amount of Stoic protreptic (persuasion) in the form of letters and essays—and it is reasonable to say that Stoicism is Lucan's idiom. One of the strongest Stoic elements in the poem is the character of Cato the Younger, whose suicide in preference to being "enslaved" (as our sources put it) by Caesar after the battle of Thapsus had made him a model of moral rectitude in Stoic thought. Lucan introduces Cato in Book 2 as wise, stern, strict, austere, and devoted to the concept of freedom; in Book 9 the trials he experiences as he leads his troops through the desert offer an allegory of the trials of the Stoic sage. Lucan would undeniably have developed Cato's role further in the rest of the poem. Suicide is another Stoic element in the poem, for example, in the strange incident of the mutual suicide of Caesar's troops on the captured raft in Book 4. The choice between living in slavery and achieving freedom in death is explicit and would probably have been developed in Lucan's treatment of Cato's suicide.

✌ *Manifestations of the supernatural*

Even without the traditional divine machinery, Lucan's poem provides plenty of supernatural phenomena. Dreams and visions, which were standard in epic and historiography too, are deployed to great effect by Lucan. As the poem survives, there are only four such episodes: Caesar's vision of Rome on the banks of the Rubicon

(1.185–203), the appearance to Pompey of his dead wife Julia (3.8–35), Pompey's dream on the night before the battle of Pharsalia at the beginning of Book 7, and the nightmares experienced by Caesar and his troops after the battle as they sleep in the Pompeians' camp (7.760–86). Even more striking are the portents, prophecies, and supernatural consultations via divination, oracles, and necromancy, with their concomitant scenes of ritual and sacrifice. For example, the final third of Book 1 and the opening third of Book 5 are both devoted to such material. Lucan uses these episodes to heighten the general level of apprehension and to create individual moments of horror. Nowhere is this more obvious than in Book 6, where Lucan's description of the witch Erichtho and her sinister rite of necromancy occupies fully half of the book. (An excerpt, 6.624–53, is included in this volume, but there is no substitute for reading the entire episode, which has remained one of the most popular parts of Lucan's poem through the centuries.) The fact that the corpse's prophecy makes up only around forty lines of an episode more than four hundred lines long (6.413–830) is proof positive that Lucan is more interested in exploring the macabre and gruesome rites than in furthering the plot. Given that there are several similar scenes in the tragedies written by his uncle Seneca at around the same time, we can safely conclude that there was an appetite for this kind of horrific material among the Roman audience of literature at this time.

◊ The protagonists in the poem

Lucan introduces his two central protagonists early in Book 1 as he weighs their ambitions, achievement, and personalities through a combination of analysis, description, and memorable imagery that depicts the energetic and younger Caesar as a thunderbolt about to strike the majestic, revered oak-tree that represents the complacent older man, Pompey (1.120–57). Neither Pompey nor Caesar can be properly called a "hero" in the conventional epic sense. Although Lucan's affection for his character Pompey shows through, his weaknesses—indecision, insecurity, reliance on the past—are on full display; he only redeems himself at the moment of death, when

he shows supreme self-control (8.618–36). Caesar is the most promi-
nent and active character in the poem as it survives. He is intro-
duced as decisive and ambitious and as reveling in war (1.143–50)
and, apart from a moment's hesitation on the banks of the Rubicon
in Book 1, his speed and military prowess make him seem invin-
cible and even quasi-divine. But that does not make him the "hero";
if anything, he is the "anti-hero." His hubristic qualities are revealed
clearly when he fells the sacred grove near Massilia (3.426–45) and
especially in the storm in Book 5, a long episode that does not ad-
vance the plot at all, but seems designed to show that Caesar thinks
that in surviving the storm he has taken on and defied the gods.
As noted above, Cato emerges as a third protagonist after Pompey's
death. In some ways he comes closest to being a "hero"—a Stoic
hero, that is, the embodiment of Stoic principles, but always one-
dimensional and never attractive. In short, Lucan has opted not to
provide a single hero, such as Odysseus or Aeneas, but instead to
create three strongly contrastive protagonists. This invites the con-
clusion that in civil war, there can be no heroes.

ᦰ The rest of the cast

Lucan deploys other characters in his poem to enhance the depic-
tions of his protagonists, to simplify what could otherwise be a
complex narrative by offering an emblem of a particular position,
and to convey the moral or emotional thrust of a scene. The women
associated with the protagonists reflect important aspects of their
characters: Marcia in Book 2 is the ascetic wife of the Stoic Cato,
while the sexy, scheming Cleopatra in Book 10 is the perfect match
for Caesar—she is another clever and ambitious tactician. Pompey's
wife Cornelia, who is certainly the most sympathetic female charac-
ter in the poem, is used by Lucan to convey Pompey's human fragil-
ity, as well as the deep loyalty that he inspires. Their mutual affection
and devotion emerge from several episodes, at the very end of Book 5
and especially in Book 8. But Pompey is also haunted by the ghost of
his previous wife, Julia, the daughter of Caesar. Lucan uses Julia to
show that Pompey can never escape his past.

Julia is also one of several manifestations of the supernatural in female form. Lucan associates the female with the supernatural starting in Book 1, with the vision of Rome in mourning and with the climactic prophecy delivered by a crazed Roman matron. In Book 5 he presents the terrifying spectacle of the Pythian priestess at the Delphic oracle being possessed by Phoebus Apollo. In Book 6, Lucan excels in his bravura display of witchcraft by Erichtho, with her supernatural powers over the dead.

The appearance of Cicero in Pompey's camp just before the battle of Pharsalia (Book 7) was noted above: the episode is certainly unhistorical, but Cicero makes a good spokesman for the senatorial viewpoint. Another unhistorical episode is the single-handed defense of Caesar's line by the centurion Scaeva in Book 6. Lucan makes Scaeva an illustration of how heroism can be perverted into a sinister superhuman force by blind devotion to Caesar's cause. While Pothinus, an adviser to Ptolemy, was a historical figure, Lucan strips his role to a single function: to advocate the assassination of a Roman general, first Pompey (Book 8) and then Caesar (Book 10). Lucan emphasizes the fact that he was a eunuch, which was not remarkable in the Egyptian court, in order to diminish his credibility and to arouse the Roman loathing of such a "half-man."

Three further minor characters are given symbolic significance that reflects features of the protagonists. Caesar's legate Curio, who appears twice in the poem (in Books 1 and 4), in Lucan's hands becomes a symbol for the corruption of Roman values in the name of ambition. Brutus is depicted as entirely devoted to Cato when he converses with him in Book 2, treating him as an oracular source of wisdom and authority; it seems likely that Lucan would have developed his character further in the rest of the poem. Finally, through the young Roman who risks his life to bury Pompey's body in Book 8 Lucan shows yet again the depth of devotion that Pompey inspires, even after his death. The youth, who is apparently Lucan's fiction, has the entirely appropriate name of Cordus, derived from the Latin word for "heart" (*cor, cordis*).

❧ Lucan as a character in his own poem

There is one further character in the poem that must be mentioned—
the poet himself. Unlike Virgil, who mostly adopts the position of the
omniscient narrator and whose interventions into his narrative are
few and far between, Lucan inserts himself repeatedly and insistently.
Right at the start, he expresses regret that Rome embroiled herself in
civil war when she might have been pursuing foreign conquests. Lu-
can's interventions are marked by the device of apostrophe, when he
directly addresses a character, or a place, in the poem. At 1.8 he ad-
dresses "Roman citizens," at 1.21 and 1.84–85 Rome, at 1.119–20 Julia,
at 1.121–24 Pompey and then Caesar, and so on. In fact, by my calcula-
tions there is one case of apostrophe every fifty-six lines on average.

Probably the most important case of apostrophe occurs near the
end of Book 9, when Lucan enters his poem to promise Caesar the
same kind of immortality that Homer bestowed on the Homeric he-
roes (9.980–86). This bold claim by the young poet is an intimation
of his own literary immortality—and here we are nearly 2000 years
later, still reading Lucan . . .

❧ Narrative momentum and delay

Just as Lucan eschews the epic norm of heroes and heroic conduct,
so too he resists the rapidity of narrative that we associate with Vir-
gil. Just as there can be no real heroes in a civil war, so too the re-
sponsible poet cannot be eager to tell his story of civil war. Lucan's
narrative technique is marked by resistance, by delay, by deferral.
Lucan's narrative technique privileges the static over the dynamic.
He allows speech to outweigh narrative and he inserts a number of
mythological episodes and scientific discussions (of geography, as-
trology, astronomy, and natural phenomena such as the snakes of
North Africa and the source of the Nile) that slow the pace and de-
fer the moment when he must depict citizen slaughtering citizen. In
this "deliberate deformation of Virgilian narrative structure" (David
Quint, *Epic and Empire* [Princeton, 1993] 134), Lucan's strategy is an
extension of his interventions into the poem: he misses no opportu-
nity to ratchet up the level of horror.

Book 1 offers a good example. Unlike Virgil, Lucan does not plunge us into the action (*in medias res*), but prefers to devote nearly two hundred lines to exploring the causes of the civil war before beginning his narrative at line 183. In a single line Lucan's Caesar has crossed the Alps, but then the narrative stops, just as soon as it has started, when Caesar is halted by a vision of Rome in mourning. In fact, the episode consists of speeches by Rome and by Caesar, then a long simile comparing Caesar to an African lion, then a description of the river Rubicon, then the narrative of the crossing (lines 220–24), and then another speech by Caesar, marking the significance of what he has just done. The proportion of narrative (i.e., material that advances the action) to non-narrative (i.e., material that delays the action) here is instructive and far from atypical. It is always valuable to assess any passage from Lucan in terms of its division between narrative and non-narrative modes.

∾ The horror of civil warfare

War was of course the staple of epic poetry, starting from Homer's *Iliad*. The epic tradition in effect prescribed certain episodes as standard, for example, catalogues of troops, preparations for battle, speeches by leaders, mass battle, heroic exploits of an individual warrior (which we label the *aristeia*, his "best" moment when he is in the spotlight), scenes of wounding, siege, fire, and the capture of a city. Lucan incorporates many of these standard features but often alters their presentation to convey his horror of civil warfare. One good example early in the poem is his description of Rome as if it were a sacked city (1.486–504): in fact, no one has invaded Rome, but the report of Caesar's rapid advance through Italy causes the people and senators alike to abandon the city. Lucan also likes to create paradoxes, such as in the sea battle off Massilia in Book 3, which soon becomes like a land battle once the ships have rammed one another. Another case of paradox is the *aristeia* of Caesar's centurion Scaeva in Book 6. In his single-handed stand against Pompey's army, Scaeva is said to be protected only by the vast number of spears stuck in his chest—and, extraordinarily, he does not die from the onslaught but reappears at the very end of our text, providing Caesar with inspiration.

Lucan's handling of violence and death likewise focuses on the horror of civil war. Most of the deaths in the poem are marked by their strangeness or suddenness and by their lack of dignity or heroism. Mutilation of bodies, living and dead, is a recurrent theme and so is burial, or lack of burial. Lucan introduces the motif of headless corpses at the end of Books 1 and 3 and also in Book 2 as a preparation for the decapitation of Pompey in Book 8. Unburied corpses torn apart by carrion crows mark the end of Book 4 and the aftermath of the battle of Pharsalia in Book 7, while Erichtho's preparations for necromancy in Book 6 show indignities inflicted on another unburied body. The makeshift burial of Pompey's headless corpse at the end of Book 8 contrasts starkly with the magnificent tomb of Alexander the Great that Caesar visits at the start of Book 10. Lucan creates horror at bodily mutilation and denial of burial as a manifestation of the breakdown of morality in civil warfare.

But it is not only the rules of humanity that are broken in civil warfare. Again and again, Lucan emphasizes that civil war involves Roman fighting Roman, brother fighting brother, father fighting son. The bonds of familial relationships are also the victims of civil war. This theme is announced before anything else, in the poem's opening line. His topic is "wars worse than civil wars." Caesar and Pompey (father-in-law and son-in-law) were not the only combatants related to one another. Hence the graphic picture of "a mighty people attacking its own guts" with the sword (lines 2–3) and hence the stark confrontation between Roman standards, Roman eagles, and Roman javelins (lines 6–7).

✙ *Lucan's Latin*

Lucan likes repetition, reiteration, and reduplication especially when, as discussed above, it allows him to slow the pace, to resist his chosen topic, and to ram home his reluctance to narrate. About one hundred years after his death, Lucan was criticized for precisely this by the orator Fronto, who was tutor to the future emperor Marcus Aurelius: "In the first seven verses at the beginning of the poem he has done nothing but paraphrase the words 'wars . . . worse than civil.' Count up the phrases in which he rings the changes on this . . . Lucan, what end will there be?" Fronto's criticism misses the point: Lucan wants his audience to stop and confront the issue.

The same motive lies behind Lucan's insertion of arresting maxims (*sententiae*) and paradoxes into his narrative. Examples from the excerpts included in this volume are *in se magna ruunt* ("mighty structures collapse onto themselves," 1.81) and *in bellum fugitur* ("they flee towards war," 1.504); there are many more. Lucan often uses *sententiae* and paradoxes to close a section, providing his audience with something to relish or puzzle over. Another delaying tactic deployed by Lucan is that of "negative enumeration"—that is, listing things that might but do not happen. A good example is the portrayal of Pompey's "funeral" in Book 8: the speech delivered over the corpse on the Egyptian shore details the features of the funeral procession of a great Roman, thereby underlining their absence.

Repetition of key words connected with the horror of civil warfare operates at the level of vocabulary and imagery too. There is a relentless recurrence of nouns and verbs denoting disintegration and destruction, on the level of the individual, the state, and the cosmos, such as *ruina* ("collapse"), *spargere* ("to scatter, break up"), and *calcare* ("to trample"), as well as *sanguis* ("blood"), *cadauera* ("corpses"), *uiscera* ("guts"), and *tabes* ("decay, putrefaction"). Panic is denoted by repetition of *praeceps* ("headlong"), *fuga* ("flight") and *fugere* ("to flee"). The guilt involved in civil war is emphasized by Lucan's insistence on *scelus* ("crime") and *nefas* ("abomination"). Lucan's choice of imagery underlines his reaction of horror. One of the most prominent strands is drawn from gladiatorial combat. Lucan uses repeated comparisons and similes to present a reversal of normal roles: instead of Romans watching barbarians and wild beasts killing one another in the arena, it is now Romans who parade their self-inflicted slaughter in front of the watching world.

Just as Lucan's style is designed to match his theme, so too his meter and his diction. In contrast with Virgil's versatile and musical handling of the hexameter, Lucan's rhythm is rather repetitive, even monotonous. His diction is prosaic, with a preference for everyday words, such as *gladius* and *cadauer*, over romantic or heroic poeticisms. Generally his range of vocabulary is limited and he avoids ornamental embellishment. Color words provide a good example: the dominant colors of the poem are black, white, and red; the glitter and shine of armor, hair, faces, sun, sea, and sky are largely absent. These choices all contribute to the stark, dark horror of civil war. Lucan is not interested in glamorizing or poeticizing the events he describes. Instead, he takes the highest genre of literature known to his culture and, rejecting, inverting, and perverting the models provided by his predecessors, makes it grimly realistic, to fit the horrific topic of Romans fighting Romans.

∾ *Suggested reading*

Introductory

Bramble, J. C. "Lucan." In *The Cambridge History of Classical Literature*, Vol. 2: *Latin Literature*, edited by E. J. Kenney and W. V. Clausen, 533–57. Cambridge, 1982.

Braund, S. H. "Introduction." In *Lucan: Civil War*, xiii–liv. Oxford World's Classics, 1992.

The poem as a whole

Ahl, F. M. *Lucan: An Introduction*. Ithaca, NY, 1976.

Bartsch, S. *Ideology in Cold Blood: A Reading of Lucan's Civil War*. Cambridge, 1997.

Behr, F. D'A. *Feeling History: Lucan, Stoicism, and the Poetics of Passion*. Columbus, OH, 2007.

Henderson, J. G. W. "Lucan: the word at war." In *Fighting for Rome: Poets and Caesars, History and Civil War*, 165–211. Cambridge, 1998.

Johnson, W. R. *Momentary Monsters: Lucan and his Heroes*. Ithaca and London, 1987.

Leigh, M. *Lucan: Spectacle and Engagement*. Oxford, 1997.

Masters, J. M. *Poetry and Civil War in Lucan's* Bellum Civile. Cambridge, 1992.

Sklenár, R. *The Taste for Nothingness. A Study of "virtus" and Related Themes in Lucan's* BELLUM CIVILE. Ann Arbor, 2003.

Particular aspects of the poem

Feeney, D. C. "*Stat magni nominis umbra*. Lucan on the greatness of Pompeius Magnus." *Classical Quarterly* 36 (1986): 239–43.

Gordon, R. "Lucan's Erictho." In *Homo Viator: Classical Essays for John Bramble*, edited by M. Whitby, P. Hardie, and M. Whitby, 231–41. Bristol and Oak Park, IL, 1987.

Grimal, P. "Is the Eulogy of Nero at the Beginning of the Pharsalia Ironic?" [Translated from French, *REL* 38 (1960): 296–305.] Forthcoming in *Oxford Readings in Lucan*, edited by C. Tesoriero. Oxford, 2009.

Lapidge, M. "Lucan's imagery of cosmic dissolution." *Hermes* 107 (1979): 344–70.

Martindale, C. A. "Paradox, hyperbole, and literary novelty in Lucan's *de Bello Civili*." *Bulletin of the Institute of Classical Studies* 23 (1976): 45–54.

———. "The Politician Lucan." *Greece & Rome* 31 (1984): 64–79.

Morford, M. P. O. *The Poet Lucan*. Oxford, 1967.

O'Hara, J. J. "Postscript: Lucan's Bellum Civile and the inconsistent Roman epic." In *Inconsistency in Roman Epic: Studies in Catullus, Lucretius, Vergil, Ovid and Lucan*, 131–42. Cambridge, 2007.

O'Higgins, D. "Lucan as *vates*." *Classical Antiquity* 7 (1988): 208–26.

Roller, M. "Ethical Contradiction and the Fractured Community in Lucan's *Bellum Civile*." *Classical Antiquity* 15 (1996): 319–47.

Lucan in the context of Roman epic

Feeney, D. C. "Epic of History: Lucan's *Bellum Civile* and *Silius' Punica*." In *The Gods in Epic: Poets and Critics of the Classical Tradition*, 250–312. Oxford, 1991.

Hardie, P. *The Epic Successors of Virgil.* Cambridge, 1993.

Martindale, C. A. *Redeeming the Text: Latin Poetry and the Hermeneutics of Reception.* Cambridge, 1993.

Quint, D. *Epic and Empire: Politics and Generic Form from Virgil to Milton.* Princeton, 1993.

Latin Text

NOTE: I retain Housman's use of consonantal **u** for authenticity, even though students find this a challenge compared with the alternative, **v**. I retain most of Housman's spellings, including **adfligo**, **inpello**, **inpius**, etc., but I have changed his **uolgus, uolnus,** and **uoltus** to **uulgus, uulnus,** and **uultus**. I use the acc. pl. form in -**es** throughout, where Housman has -**is**.

Specific divergences from his text and punctuation are the following:

1.16	**oris** for **horis**
1.18	**Pontum** for **pontum**
1.495	**Vrbem** for **urbem**
1.503	**Vrbe** for **urbe**
3.435	**telo** for **ferro**
6.637	**pectore** for **gutture**
6.638	**ducitur** for **ducit et**
7.658	**fouit** for **uouit**
7.666	question mark for period after **meum**
7.730	comma added after **ratus**
7.734	**Fortuna** for **fortuna**
7.768	**nocentes** for **nocentem**
7.810	**Natura** for **natura**
8.562	**longe** for **longa**
8.563	**adpellat** for **appulerat**
8.665	**placatam** for **iratam**
9.215	comma removed after **maior**
9.216	comma removed after **laudes**

∾ *1.1–45*

Bella per Emathios plus quam ciuilia campos
iusque datum sceleri canimus, populumque potentem
in sua uictrici conuersum uiscera dextra
cognatasque acies, et rupto foedere regni
5 certatum totis concussi uiribus orbis
in commune nefas, infestisque obuia signis
signa, pares aquilas et pila minantia pilis.
   quis furor, o ciues, quae tanta licentia ferri?
gentibus inuisis Latium praebere cruorem
10 cumque superba foret Babylon spolianda tropaeis
Ausoniis umbraque erraret Crassus inulta
bella geri placuit nullos habitura triumphos?
heu, quantum terrae potuit pelagique parari
hoc quem ciuiles hauserunt sanguine dextrae,
15 unde uenit Titan et nox ubi sidera condit
quaque dies medius flagrantibus aestuat oris
et qua bruma rigens ac nescia uere remitti
astringit Scythico glacialem frigore Pontum!
sub iuga iam Seres, iam barbarus isset Araxes
20 et gens siqua iacet nascenti conscia Nilo.
tum, si tantus amor belli tibi, Roma, nefandi,
totum sub Latias leges cum miseris orbem,
in te uerte manus: nondum tibi defuit hostis.
at nunc semirutis pendent quod moenia tectis
25 urbibus Italiae lapsisque ingentia muris
saxa iacent nulloque domus custode tenentur
rarus et antiquis habitator in urbibus errat,

horrida quod dumis multosque inarata per annos

Hesperia est desuntque manus poscentibus aruis,

30   non tu, Pyrrhe ferox, nec tantis cladibus auctor

Poenus erit: nulli penitus descendere ferro

contigit; alta sedent ciuilis uulnera dextrae.

quod si non aliam uenturo fata Neroni

inuenere uiam magnoque aeterna parantur

35   regna deis caelumque suo seruire Tonanti

non nisi saeuorum potuit post bella gigantum,

iam nihil, o superi, querimur; scelera ipsa nefasque

hac mercede placent. diros Pharsalia campos

inpleat et Poeni saturentur sanguine manes,

40   ultima funesta concurrant proelia Munda,

his, Caesar, Perusina fames Mutinaeque labores

accedant fatis et quas premit aspera classes

Leucas et ardenti seruilia bella sub Aetna,

multum Roma tamen debet ciuilibus armis

quod tibi res acta est.

ꙮ *1.67–157*

fert animus causas tantarum expromere rerum,

inmensumque aperitur opus, quid in arma furentem

inpulerit populum, quid pacem excusserit orbi.

70   inuida fatorum series summisque negatum

stare diu nimioque graues sub pondere lapsus

nec se Roma ferens. sic, cum conpage soluta

saecula tot mundi suprema coegerit hora

75/76 antiquum repetens iterum chaos, ignea pontum

astra petent, tellus extendere litora nolet
excutietque fretum, fratri contraria Phoebe
ibit et obliquum bigas agitare per orbem
indignata diem poscet sibi, totaque discors
80   machina diuolsi turbabit foedera mundi.
in se magna ruunt: laetis hunc numina rebus
crescendi posuere modum. nec gentibus ullis
commodat in populum terrae pelagique potentem
inuidiam Fortuna suam. tu causa malorum
85   facta tribus dominis communis, Roma, nec umquam
in turbam missi feralia foedera regni.
o male concordes nimiaque cupidine caeci,
quid miscere iuuat uires orbemque tenere
in medio? dum terra fretum terramque leuabit
90   aer et longi uoluent Titana labores
noxque diem caelo totidem per signa sequetur,
nulla fides regni sociis, omnisque potestas
inpatiens consortis erit. nec gentibus ullis
credite nec longe fatorum exempla petantur:
95   fraterno primi maduerunt sanguine muri.
nec pretium tanti tellus pontusque furoris
tunc erat: exiguum dominos commisit asylum.
   temporis angusti mansit concordia discors
paxque fuit non sponte ducum; nam sola futuri
100   Crassus erat belli medius mora. qualiter undas
qui secat et geminum gracilis mare separat Isthmos
nec patitur conferre fretum, si terra recedat,
Ionium Aegaeo frangat mare, sic, ubi saeua

arma ducum dirimens miserando funere Crassus
105 Assyrias Latio maculauit sanguine Carrhas,
Parthica Romanos soluerunt damna furores.
plus illa uobis acie, quam creditis, actum est,
Arsacidae: bellum uictis ciuile dedistis.
diuiditur ferro regnum, populique potentis,
110 quae mare, quae terras, quae totum possidet orbem,
non cepit fortuna duos. nam pignora iuncti
sanguinis et diro ferales omine taedas
abstulit ad manes Parcarum Iulia saeua
intercepta manu. quod si tibi fata dedissent
115 maiores in luce moras, tu sola furentem
inde uirum poteras atque hinc retinere parentem
armatasque manus excusso iungere ferro,
ut generos soceris mediae iunxere Sabinae.
morte tua discussa fides bellumque mouere
120 permissum ducibus. stimulos dedit aemula uirtus.
tu, noua ne ueteres obscurent acta triumphos
et uictis cedat piratica laurea Gallis,
Magne, times; te iam series ususque laborum
erigit inpatiensque loci fortuna secundi;
125 nec quemquam iam ferre potest Caesarue priorem
Pompeiusue parem. quis iustius induit arma
scire nefas: magno se iudice quisque tuetur;
uictrix causa deis placuit sed uicta Catoni.
nec coiere pares. alter uergentibus annis
130 in senium longoque togae tranquillior usu
dedidicit iam pace ducem, famaeque petitor

multa dare in uulgus, totus popularibus auris
inpelli plausuque sui gaudere theatri,
nec reparare nouas uires, multumque priori
135 credere fortunae. stat magni nominis umbra,
qualis frugifero quercus sublimis in agro
exuuias ueteris populi sacrataque gestans
dona ducum nec iam ualidis radicibus haerens
pondere fixa suo est, nudosque per aera ramos
140 effundens trunco, non frondibus, efficit umbram,
et quamuis primo nutet casura sub Euro,
tot circum siluae firmo se robore tollant,
sola tamen colitur. sed non in Caesare tantum
nomen erat nec fama ducis, sed nescia uirtus
145 stare loco, solusque pudor non uincere bello.
acer et indomitus, quo spes quoque ira uocasset,
ferre manum et numquam temerando parcere ferro,
successus urguere suos, instare fauori
numinis, inpellens quidquid sibi summa petenti
150 obstaret gaudensque uiam fecisse ruina,
qualiter expressum uentis per nubila fulmen
aetheris inpulsi sonitu mundique fragore
emicuit rupitque diem populosque pauentes
terruit obliqua praestringens lumina flamma:
155 in sua templa furit, nullaque exire uetante
materia magnamque cadens magnamque reuertens
dat stragem late sparsosque recolligit ignes.

[Removed from Book 1: 75–76 omnia mixtis | sidera sideribus con-
current]

∾ *1.183–227*

iam gelidas Caesar cursu superauerat Alpes
ingentisque animo motus bellumque futurum
185 ceperat. ut uentum est parui Rubiconis ad undas,
ingens uisa duci patriae trepidantis imago
clara per obscuram uoltu maestissima noctem
turrigero canos effundens uertice crines
caesarie lacera nudisque adstare lacertis
190 et gemitu permixta loqui: 'quo tenditis ultra?
quo fertis mea signa, uiri? si iure uenitis,
si ciues, huc usque licet.' tum perculit horror
membra ducis, riguere comae gressumque coercens
languor in extrema tenuit uestigia ripa.
195 mox ait 'o magnae qui moenia prospicis urbis
Tarpeia de rupe Tonans Phrygiique penates
gentis Iuleae et rapti secreta Quirini
et residens celsa Latiaris Iuppiter Alba
Vestalesque foci summique o numinis instar
200 Roma, faue coeptis. non te furialibus armis
persequor: en, adsum uictor terraque marique
Caesar, ubique tuus (liceat modo, nunc quoque) miles.
ille erit ille nocens, qui me tibi fecerit hostem.'
inde moras soluit belli tumidumque per amnem
205 signa tulit propere: sicut squalentibus aruis
aestiferae Libyes uiso leo comminus hoste
subsedit dubius, totam dum colligit iram;
mox, ubi se saeuae stimulauit uerbere caudae
erexitque iubam et uasto graue murmur hiatu

210 infremuit, tum torta leuis si lancea Mauri
    haereat aut latum subeant uenabula pectus,
    per ferrum tanti securus uulneris exit.

        fonte cadit modico paruisque inpellitur undis
    puniceus Rubicon, cum feruida canduit aestas,
215 perque imas serpit ualles et Gallica certus
    limes ab Ausoniis disterminat arua colonis.
    tum uires praebebat hiemps atque auxerat undas
    tertia iam grauido pluuialis Cynthia cornu
    et madidis Euri resolutae flatibus Alpes.
220 primus in obliquum sonipes opponitur amnem
    excepturus aquas; molli tum cetera rumpit
    turba uado faciles iam fracti fluminis undas.
    Caesar, ut aduersam superato gurgite ripam
    attigit, Hesperiae uetitis et constitit aruis,
225 'hic' ait 'hic pacem temerataque iura relinquo;
    te, Fortuna, sequor. procul hinc iam foedera sunto;
    credidimus satis <his>, utendum est iudice bello.'

∾ *1.486–504*

                        nec solum uulgus inani
    percussum terrore pauet, sed curia et ipsi
    sedibus exiluere patres, inuisaque belli
    consulibus fugiens mandat decreta senatus.
490 tum, quae tuta petant et quae metuenda relinquant
    incerti, quo quemque fugae tulit impetus urguent
    praecipitem populum, serieque haerentia longa
    agmina prorumpunt. credas aut tecta nefandas

corripuisse faces aut iam quatiente ruina
495 nutantes pendere domos, sic turba per Vrbem
praecipiti lymphata gradu, uelut unica rebus
spes foret adflictis patrios excedere muros,
inconsulta ruit. qualis, cum turbidus Auster
reppulit a Libycis inmensum Syrtibus aequor
500 fractaque ueliferi sonuerunt pondera mali,
desilit in fluctus deserta puppe magister
nauitaque et nondum sparsa conpage carinae
naufragium sibi quisque facit, sic Vrbe relicta
in bellum fugitur.

❧ 3.8–35

inde soporifero cesserunt languida somno
membra ducis; diri tum plena horroris imago
10 uisa caput maestum per hiantis Iulia terras
tollere et accenso furialis stare sepulchro.
'sedibus Elysiis campoque expulsa piorum
ad Stygias' inquit 'tenebras manesque nocentes
post bellum ciuile trahor. uidi ipsa tenentes
15 Eumenidas quaterent quas uestris lampadas armis;
praeparat innumeras puppes Acherontis adusti
portitor; in multas laxantur Tartara poenas;
uix operi cunctae dextra properante sorores
sufficiunt, lassant rumpentis stamina Parcas.
20 coniuge me laetos duxisti, Magne, triumphos:
fortuna est mutata toris, semperque potentes
detrahere in cladem fato damnata maritos

innupsit tepido paelex Cornelia busto.

haereat illa tuis per bella per aequora signis,

25   dum non securos liceat mihi rumpere somnos

et nullum uestro uacuum sit tempus amori

sed teneat Caesarque dies et Iulia noctes.

me non Lethaeae, coniunx, obliuia ripae

inmemorem fecere tui, regesque silentum

30   permisere sequi. ueniam te bella gerente

in medias acies. numquam tibi, Magne, per umbras

perque meos manes genero non esse licebit;

abscidis frustra ferro tua pignora: bellum

te faciet ciuile meum.' sic fata refugit

35   umbra per amplexus trepidi dilapsa mariti.

∾ 3.399–445

lucus erat longo numquam uiolatus ab aeuo

400 obscurum cingens conexis aera ramis

et gelidas alte summotis solibus umbras.

hunc non ruricolae Panes nemorumque potentes

Siluani Nymphaeque tenent, sed barbara ritu

sacra deum; structae diris altaribus arae

405 omnisque humanis lustrata cruoribus arbor.

siqua fidem meruit superos mirata uetustas,

illis et uolucres metuunt insistere ramis

et lustris recubare ferae; nec uentus in illas

incubuit siluas excussaque nubibus atris

410 fulgura: non ulli frondem praebentibus aurae

arboribus suus horror inest. tum plurima nigris

fontibus unda cadit, simulacraque maesta deorum

arte carent caesisque extant informia truncis.

ipse situs putrique facit iam robore pallor

415 attonitos; non uulgatis sacrata figuris

numina sic metuunt: tantum terroribus addit,

quos timeant, non nosse, deos. iam fama ferebat

saepe cauas motu terrae mugire cauernas,

et procumbentes iterum consurgere taxos,

420 et non ardentis fulgere incendia siluae,

roboraque amplexos circum fluxisse dracones.

non illum cultu populi propiore frequentant

sed cessere deis. medio cum Phoebus in axe est

aut caelum nox atra tenet, pauet ipse sacerdos

425 accessus dominumque timet deprendere luci.

   hanc iubet inmisso siluam procumbere ferro;

nam uicina operi belloque intacta priore

inter nudatos stabat densissima montis.

sed fortes tremuere manus, motique uerenda

430 maiestate loci, si robora sacra ferirent,

in sua credebant reditras membra securis.

inplicitas magno Caesar torpore cohortes

ut uidit, primus raptam librare bipennem

ausus et aeriam ferro proscindere quercum

435 effatur merso uiolata in robora telo

'iam nequis uestrum dubitet subuertere siluam

credite me fecisse nefas.' tum paruit omnis

imperiis non sublato secura pauore

turba, sed expensa superorum et Caesaris ira.

440 procumbunt orni, nodosa inpellitur ilex,
    siluaque Dodones et fluctibus aptior alnus
    et non plebeios luctus testata cupressus
    tum primum posuere comas et fronde carentes
    admisere diem, propulsaque robore denso
445 sustinuit se silua cadens.

∾ 6.624–53

    dixerat, et noctis geminatis arte tenebris
625 maestum tecta caput squalenti nube pererrat
    corpora caesorum tumulis proiecta negatis.
    continuo fugere lupi, fugere reuolsis
    unguibus inpastae uolucres, dum Thessala uatem
    eligit et gelidas leto scrutata medullas
630 pulmonis rigidi stantes sine uulnere fibras
    inuenit et uocem defuncto in corpore quaerit.
    fata peremptorum pendent iam multa uirorum,
    quem superis reuocasse uelit. si tollere totas
    temptasset campis acies et reddere bello,
635 cessissent leges Erebi, monstroque potenti
    extractus Stygio populus pugnasset Auerno.
    electum tandem traiecto pectore corpus
    ducitur inserto laqueis feralibus unco
    per scopulos miserum trahitur per saxa cadauer
640 uicturum, montisque caui, quem tristis Erictho
    damnarat sacris, alta sub rupe locatur.
        haud procul a Ditis caecis depressa cauernis
    in praeceps subsedit humus, quam pallida pronis

urguet silua comis et nullo uertice caelum
645 suspiciens Phoebo non peruia taxus opacat.
marcentes intus tenebrae pallensque sub antris
longa nocte situs numquam nisi carmine factum
lumen habet. non Taenariis sic faucibus aer
sedit iners, maestum mundi confine latentis
650 ac nostri, quo non metuant admittere manes
Tartarei reges. nam, quamuis Thessala uates
uim faciat fatis, dubium est, quod traxerit illuc
aspiciat Stygias an quod descenderit umbras.

❧ 7.617–37

inpendisse pudet lacrimas in funere mundi
mortibus innumeris, ac singula fata sequentem
quaerere letiferum per cuius uiscera uulnus
620 exierit, quis fusa solo uitalia calcet,
ore quis aduerso demissum faucibus ensem
expulerit moriens anima, quis corruat ictus,
quis steterit dum membra cadunt, qui pectore tela
transmittant aut quos campis adfixerit hasta,
625 quis cruor emissis perruperit aera uenis
inque hostis cadat arma sui, quis pectora fratris
caedat et, ut notum possit spoliare cadauer,
abscisum longe mittat caput, ora parentis
quis laceret nimiaque probet spectantibus ira
630 quem iugulat non esse patrem. mors nulla querella
digna sua est, nullosque hominum lugere uacamus.
non istas habuit pugnae Pharsalia partes

quas aliae clades: illic per fata uirorum,

per populos hic Roma perit; quod militis illic,

635   mors hic gentis erat: sanguis ibi fluxit Achaeus,

Ponticus, Assyrius; cunctos haerere cruores

Romanus campisque uetat consistere torrens.

∾ 7.647–82

iam Magnus transisse deos Romanaque fata

senserat infelix, tota uix clade coactus

fortunam damnare suam. stetit aggere campi,

650   eminus unde omnes sparsas per Thessala rura

aspiceret clades, quae bello obstante latebant.

tot telis sua fata peti, tot corpora fusa

ac se tam multo pereuntem sanguine uidit.

nec, sicut mos est miseris, trahere omnia secum

655   mersa iuuat gentesque suae miscere ruinae:

ut Latiae post se uiuat pars maxima turbae,

sustinuit dignos etiamnunc credere uotis

caelicolas, fouitque sui solacia casus.

'parcite,' ait 'superi, cunctas prosternere gentes.

660   stante potest mundo Romaque superstite Magnus

esse miser. si plura iuuant mea uulnera, coniunx

est mihi, sunt nati: dedimus tot pignora fatis.

ciuiline parum est bello, si meque meosque

obruit? exiguae clades sumus orbe remoto?

665   omnia quid laceras? quid perdere cuncta laboras?

iam nihil est, Fortuna, meum?' sic fatur et arma

signaque et adflictas omni iam parte cateruas

circumit et reuocat matura in fata ruentes

seque negat tanti. nec derat robur in enses

670 ire duci iuguloque pati uel pectore letum.

sed timuit, strato miles ne corpore Magni

non fugeret, supraque ducem procumberet orbis;

Caesaris aut oculis uoluit subducere mortem.

nequiquam, infelix: socero spectare uolenti

675 praestandum est ubicumque caput. sed tu quoque, coniunx,

causa fugae uultusque tui fatisque negatum

parte absente mori. tum Magnum concitus aufert

a bello sonipes non tergo tela pauentem

ingentesque animos extrema in fata ferentem.

680 non gemitus, non fletus erat, saluaque uerendus

maiestate dolor, qualem te, Magne, decebat

Romanis praestare malis.

∾ 7.728–46

Caesar, ut Hesperio uidit satis arua natare

sanguine, parcendum ferro manibusque suorum

730 iam ratus, ut uiles animas perituraque frustra

agmina permisit uitae. sed, castra fugatos

ne reuocent pellatque quies nocturna pauorem,

protinus hostili statuit succedere uallo,

dum Fortuna calet, dum conficit omnia terror,

735 non ueritus graue ne fessis aut Marte subactis

hoc foret imperium. non magno hortamine miles

in praedam ducendus erat. 'uictoria nobis

plena, uiri:' dixit 'superest pro sanguine merces,

quam monstrare meum est; neque enim donare uocabo
740 quod sibi quisque dabit. cunctis, en, plena metallis
castra patent; raptum Hesperiis e gentibus aurum
hic iacet Eoasque premunt tentoria gazas.
tot regum fortuna simul Magnique coacta
expectat dominos: propera praecedere, miles,
745 quos sequeris; quascumque tuas Pharsalia fecit
a uictis rapiuntur opes.'

～ *7.760–811*

760   capit inpia plebes
caespite patricio somnos, stratumque cubile
regibus infandus miles premit, inque parentum
inque toris fratrum posuerunt membra nocentes.
quos agitat uaesana quies, somnique furentes
765 Thessalicam miseris uersant in pectore pugnam.
inuigilat cunctis saeuum scelus, armaque tota
mente agitant, capuloque manus absente mouentur.
ingemuisse putem campos, terramque nocentes
inspirasse animas, infectumque aera totum
770 manibus et superam Stygia formidine noctem.
exigit a meritis tristes uictoria poenas,
sibilaque et flammas infert sopor. umbra perempti
ciuis adest; sua quemque premit terroris imago:
ille senum uultus, iuuenum uidet ille figuras,
775 hunc agitant totis fraterna cadauera somnis,
pectore in hoc pater est, omnes in Caesare manes.
haud alios nondum Scythica purgatus in ara

Eumenidum uidit uultus Pelopeus Orestes,

nec magis attonitos animi sensere tumultus,

780 cum fureret Pentheus aut, cum desisset, Agaue.

hunc omnes gladii, quos aut Pharsalia uidit

aut ultrix uisura dies stringente senatu,

illa nocte premunt, hunc infera monstra flagellant.

et quantum poenae misero mens conscia donat,

785 quod Styga, quod manes ingestaque Tartara somnis

Pompeio uiuente uidet! tamen omnia passo,

postquam clara dies Pharsalica damna retexit,

nulla loci facies reuocat feralibus aruis

haerentes oculos. cernit propulsa cruore

790 flumina et excelsos cumulis aequantia colles

corpora, sidentes in tabem spectat aceruos

et Magni numerat populos, epulisque paratur

ille locus, uultus ex quo faciesque iacentum

agnoscat. iuuat Emathiam non cernere terram

795 et lustrare oculis campos sub clade latentes.

fortunam superosque suos in sanguine cernit.

ac, ne laeta furens scelerum spectacula perdat,

inuidet igne rogi miseris, caeloque nocenti

ingerit Emathiam. non illum Poenus humator

800 consulis et Libyca succensae lampade Cannae

conpellunt hominum ritus ut seruet in hoste,

sed meminit nondum satiata caedibus ira

ciues esse suos. petimus non singula busta

discretosque rogos: unum da gentibus ignem,

805 non interpositis urantur corpora flammis;

aut, generi si poena iuuat, nemus extrue Pindi,
erige congestas Oetaeo robore siluas,
Thessalicam uideat Pompeius ab aequore flammam.
nil agis hac ira: tabesne cadauera soluat
810   an rogus, haud refert; placido Natura receptat
cuncta sinu, finemque sui sibi corpora debent.

∾ *8.542–636*

o superi, Nilusne et barbara Memphis
et Pelusiaci tam mollis turba Canopi
hos animos? sic fata premunt ciuilia mundum?
545   sic Romana iacent? ullusne in cladibus istis
est locus Aegypto Phariusque admittitur ensis?
hanc certe seruate fidem, ciuilia bella:
cognatas praestate manus externaque monstra
pellite, si meruit tam claro nomine Magnus
550   Caesaris esse nefas. tanti, Ptolemaee, ruinam
nominis haut metuis, caeloque tonante profanas
inseruisse manus, inpure ac semiuir, audes?
non domitor mundi nec ter Capitolia curru
inuectus regumque potens uindexque senatus
555   uictorisque gener, Phario satis esse tyranno
quod poterat, Romanus erat: quid uiscera nostra
scrutaris gladio? nescis, puer inprobe, nescis
quo tua sit fortuna loco: iam iure sine ullo
Nili sceptra tenes; cecidit ciuilibus armis
560   qui tibi regna dedit. iam uento uela negarat
Magnus et auxilio remorum infanda petebat

litora; quem contra non longe uecta biremi
adpellat scelerata manus, Magnoque patere
fingens regna Phari celsae de puppe carinae
565 in paruam iubet ire ratem, litusque malignum
incusat bimaremque uadis frangentibus aestum,
qui uetet externas terris adpellere classes.
quod nisi fatorum leges intentaque iussu
ordinis aeterni miserae uicinia mortis
570 damnatum leto traherent ad litora Magnum,
non ulli comitum sceleris praesagia derant:
quippe, fides si pura foret, si regia Magno
sceptrorum auctori uera pietate pateret,
uenturum tota Pharium cum classe tyrannum.
575 sed cedit fatis classemque relinquere iussus
obsequitur, letumque iuuat praeferre timori.
ibat in hostilem praeceps Cornelia puppem,
hoc magis inpatiens egresso desse marito
quod metuit clades. 'remane, temeraria coniunx,
580 et tu, nate, precor, longeque a litore casus
expectate meos et in hac ceruice tyranni
explorate fidem' dixit. sed surda uetanti
tendebat geminas amens Cornelia palmas.
'quo sine me crudelis abis? iterumne relinquor,
585 Thessalicis summota malis? numquam omine laeto
distrahimur miseri. poteras non flectere puppem,
cum fugeres alto, latebrisque relinquere Lesbi,
omnibus a terris si nos arcere parabas.
an tantum in fluctus placeo comes?' haec ubi frustra

590   effudit, prima pendet tamen anxia puppe,
       attonitoque metu nec quoquam auertere uisus
       nec Magnum spectare potest. stetit anxia classis
       ad ducis euentum, metuens non arma nefasque
       sed ne summissis precibus Pompeius adoret
595   sceptra sua donata manu. transire parantem
       Romanus Pharia miles de puppe salutat
       Septimius, qui, pro superum pudor, arma satelles
       regia gestabat posito deformia pilo,
       inmanis uiolentus atrox nullaque ferarum
600   mitior in caedes. quis non, Fortuna, putasset
       parcere te populis, quod bello haec dextra uacaret
       Thessaliaque procul tam noxia tela fugasses?
       disponis gladios, nequo non fiat in orbe,
       heu, facinus ciuile tibi. uictoribus ipsis
605   dedecus et numquam superum caritura pudore
       fabula, Romanus regi sic paruit ensis,
       Pellaeusque puer gladio tibi colla recidit,
       Magne, tuo. qua posteritas in saecula mittet
       Septimium fama? scelus hoc quo nomine dicent
610   qui Bruti dixere nefas? iam uenerat horae
       terminus extremae, Phariamque ablatus in alnum
       perdiderat iam iura sui. tum stringere ferrum
       regia monstra parant. ut uidit comminus enses,
       inuoluit uultus atque, indignatus apertum
615   fortunae praebere, caput; tum lumina pressit
       continuitque animam, nequas effundere uoces
       uellet et aeternam fletu corrumpere famam.

      sed, postquam mucrone latus funestus Achillas

      perfodit, nullo gemitu consensit ad ictum

620 respexitque nefas, seruatque inmobile corpus,

      seque probat moriens atque haec in pectore uoluit:

      'saecula Romanos numquam tacitura labores

      attendunt, aeuumque sequens speculatur ab omni

      orbe ratem Phariamque fidem: nunc consule famae.

625 fata tibi longae fluxerunt prospera uitae:

      ignorant populi, si non in morte probaris,

      an scieris aduersa pati. ne cede pudori

      auctoremque dole fati: quacumque feriris,

      crede manum soceri. spargant lacerentque licebit,

630 sum tamen, o superi, felix, nullique potestas

      hoc auferre deo. mutantur prospera uita,

      non fit morte miser. uidet hanc Cornelia caedem

      Pompeiusque meus: tanto patientius, oro,

      claude, dolor, gemitus: gnatus coniunxque peremptum,

635 si mirantur, amant.' talis custodia Magno

      mentis erat, ius hoc animi morientis habebat.

❧ 8.663–88

      at, Magni cum terga sonent et pectora ferro,

      permansisse decus sacrae uenerabile formae

665 placatamque deis faciem, nil ultima mortis

      ex habitu uultuque uiri mutasse fatentur

      qui lacerum uidere caput. nam saeuus in ipso

      Septimius sceleris maius scelus inuenit actu,

      ac retegit sacros scisso uelamine uultus

670 semianimis Magni spirantiaque occupat ora
     collaque in obliquo ponit languentia transtro.
     tunc neruos uenasque secat nodosaque frangit
     ossa diu: nondum artis erat caput ense rotare.
     at, postquam trunco ceruix abscisa recessit,
675 uindicat hoc Pharius, dextra gestare, satelles.
     degener atque operae miles Romane secundae,
     Pompei diro sacrum caput ense recidis,
     ut non ipse feras? o summi fata pudoris!
     inpius ut Magnum nosset puer, illa uerenda
680 regibus hirta coma et generosa fronte decora
     caesaries conprensa manu est, Pharioque ueruto,
     dum uiuunt uultus atque os in murmura pulsant
     singultus animae, dum lumina nuda rigescunt,
     suffixum caput est, quo numquam bella iubente
685 pax fuit; hoc leges Campumque et rostra mouebat,
     hac facie, Fortuna, tibi, Romana, placebas.
     nec satis infando fuit hoc uidisse tyranno:
     uult sceleris superesse fidem.

∿ *9.190–217*

190 'ciuis obit' inquit 'multum maioribus inpar
     nosse modum iuris, sed in hoc tamen utilis aeuo,
     cui non ulla fuit iusti reuerentia; salua
     libertate potens, et solus plebe parata
     priuatus seruire sibi, rectorque senatus,
195 sed regnantis, erat. nil belli iure poposcit,
     quaeque dari uoluit uoluit sibi posse negari.

inmodicas possedit opes, sed plura retentis

intulit. inuasit ferrum, sed ponere norat.

praetulit arma togae, sed pacem armatus amauit.

200 iuuit sumpta ducem, iuuit dimissa potestas.

casta domus luxuque carens corruptaque numquam

fortuna domini. clarum et uenerabile nomen

gentibus et multum nostrae quod proderat urbi.

olim uera fides Sulla Marioque receptis

205 libertatis obit: Pompeio rebus adempto

nunc et ficta perit. non iam regnare pudebit,

nec color imperii nec frons erit ulla senatus.

o felix, cui summa dies fuit obuia uicto

et cui quaerendos Pharium scelus obtulit enses.

210 forsitan in soceri potuisses uiuere regno.

scire mori sors prima uiris, set proxima cogi.

et mihi, si fatis aliena in iura uenimus,

fac talem, Fortuna, Iubam; non deprecor hosti

seruari, dum me seruet ceruice recisa.'

215   uocibus his maior quam si Romana sonarent

rostra ducis laudes generosam uenit ad umbram

mortis honos.

∾ *9.961–99*

Sigeasque petit famae mirator harenas

et Simoentis aquas et Graio nobile busto

Rhoetion et multum debentes uatibus umbras.

circumit exustae nomen memorabile Troiae

965 magnaque Phoebei quaerit uestigia muri.

iam siluae steriles et putres robore trunci
Assaraci pressere domos et templa deorum
iam lassa radice tenent, ac tota teguntur
Pergama dumetis: etiam periere ruinae.

970 aspicit Hesiones scopulos siluaque latentes
Anchisae thalamos; quo iudex sederit antro,
unde puer raptus caelo, quo uertice Nais
luxerit Oenone: nullum est sine nomine saxum.
inscius in sicco serpentem puluere riuum

975 transierat, qui Xanthus erat. securus in alto
gramine ponebat gressus: Phryx incola manes
Hectoreos calcare uetat. discussa iacebant
saxa nec ullius faciem seruantia sacri:
'Herceas' monstrator ait 'non respicis aras?'

980   o sacer et magnus uatum labor! omnia fato
eripis et populis donas mortalibus aeuum.
inuidia sacrae, Caesar, ne tangere famae;
nam, siquid Latiis fas est promittere Musis,
quantum Zmyrnaei durabunt uatis honores,

985 uenturi me teque legent; Pharsalia nostra
uiuet, et a nullo tenebris damnabimur aeuo.
   ut ducis inpleuit uisus ueneranda uetustas,
erexit subitas congestu caespitis aras
uotaque turicremos non inrita fudit in ignes.

990 'di cinerum, Phrygias colitis quicumque ruinas,
Aeneaeque mei, quos nunc Lauinia sedes
seruat et Alba, lares, et quorum lucet in aris
ignis adhuc Phrygius, nullique aspecta uirorum

Pallas, in abstruso pignus memorabile templo,

995 gentis Iuleae uestris clarissimus aris

dat pia tura nepos et uos in sede priore

rite uocat. date felices in cetera cursus,

restituam populos; grata uice moenia reddent

Ausonidae Phrygibus, Romanaque Pergama surgent.'

∾ *Eastern Mediterranean in Caesar's Day*

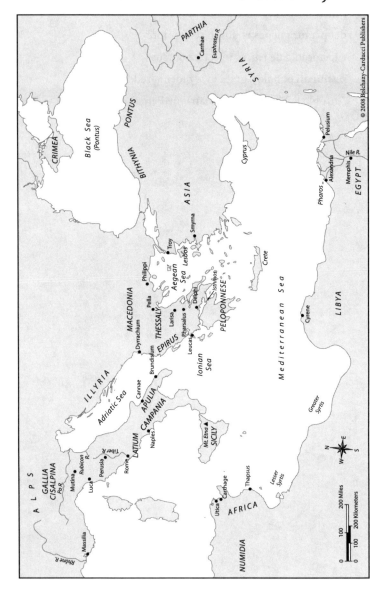

Commentary
❧ *Lucan's theme, 1.1–45*

Lucan states the theme of his poem (1–7), the civil war between Caesar and Pompey, which he describes as "worse than civil war" because the two leaders were related to one another by marriage. He then expresses regret about Rome's embroilment in civil war when she might have been conquering the rest of the world (8–32). But he declares that the civil war and other terrible events which followed were worthwhile if the result was to have Nero as emperor (33–45).

1   **bella** the conventional topic of epic poetry, but later in the line Lucan qualifies these "wars" not as "civil wars" but as "worse (lit. "more") than civil wars," thereby delivering a surprise right at the start of his poem.

Emathios . . . campos technically Emathia was in Macedonia, but Lucan uses the adjective to mean Thessaly, the location of the battle of Pharsalia, the main battle of the civil war.

plus quam ciuilia because the protagonists, Caesar and Pompey, are not only fellow Roman citizens but also related to one another by marriage, hence they will sometimes be called "father-in-law" and "son-in-law."

2   **ius** "law," "legality"

canimus by convention epic poets use the plural.

3   This is the first case of a "Golden Line" in Lucan's epic, a modern name given to a line with the balanced pattern abVAB, where a and b are adjectives that qualify nouns A and B, flanking the verb (here a pf. participle) in central position. It is typical of Lucan to deploy formal perfection in combination with distressing or gruesome ideas, as here.

in sua . . . uiscera *in* + acc., "into," after *conuersum*

uictrici . . . dextra "victorious" over the rest of the world; the "right hand" denotes the sword hand.

4 **rupto foedere** abl. absolute

foedere regni "the pact of tyranny" was the so-called first triumvirate, a pact made in 60 BCE, in which Pompey, Caesar, and Crassus agreed to cooperate politically with one another; this arrangement broke down in the late 50s; the word *regnum* makes the Roman state a "kingdom" not a republic, with all the accompanying negative associations about kings in Roman thought.

5 **certatum** in effect, "the struggle"; the n. sing. pf. pass. participle is used substantivally; cf. *negatum* (70)

orbis Lucan identifies the Roman conflict as one which affects the entire world.

6 **in commune nefas** lit. "towards a shared crime," i.e., "for universal guilt": Lucan is saying that everyone who participates in the civil war is committing a "crime." *nefas* is a key word in the poem as Lucan condemns the civil war; it denotes the contravention of divine law and etymologically it may derive from the verb *for, fari*, "to speak"; if that is correct, Lucan as poet puts himself in the impossible position of speaking "the unspeakable."

6-7 Lucan finds three different ways of depicting Roman battle line facing Roman battle line, by mentioning three distinctively Roman items: the standards (*signa*), the eagles (*aquilae*) and the javelins (*pila*). Further, the idea that *signa* might be aggressively facing (*obuia*) "hostile" (*infestis*) *signa* is designed to be shocking.

7 **aquilas** each Roman legion had an eagle as its standard.

pila n. pl.; the *pilum*, a javelin or throwing-spear, was the distinctive weapon of the Roman legionary soldier.

8 **quis . . . quae . . . ?** the question words assume a verb such as *fuit*.

o ciues this is the first example in the poem of apostrophe, i.e., when Lucan directly addresses a character or place in the poem; it is a technique he deploys very frequently and it means that we are more aware of the authorial voice than usual in Greco-Roman epic poetry.

tanta licentia ferri "excessive freedom with the sword" (lit. "of the sword"); *licentia* is usually negative; *ferrum*, lit. "iron," metonymically = the item made from iron, here "sword."

9   **gentibus inuisis** dat. after *praebere*; the foreign nations surrounding the Roman empire

Latium "Latian" means "Roman," as often, referring to Latium, the area of Italy in which Rome was located.

praebere cruorem the infinitive is parallel to *bella geri* (12), connected by *-que* after *cum*, and both infinitives follow *placuit* (12).

10   **foret . . . spolianda** periphrastic gerundive, expressing an imperative, "ought to be stripped"

Babylon a city in Parthia

10-11 **tropaeis Ausoniis** abl. of deprivation; the "Ausonian trophies" were the Roman standards recently lost to the Parthians by Crassus at the battle of Carrhae in 53 BCE; Lucan asserts that these should have been recovered before the Romans indulged in civil war. *Ausonia* = Italy, hence "Ausonian" can mean "Italian" or "Roman."

11   **umbra . . . inulta** abl.; Crassus died at the battle of Carrhae.

12   **bella geri** lit. "that wars be waged"

placuit supply *uobis*, i.e., "to you citizens"

nullos habitura triumphos *habitura* is fut. participle expanding on *bella*, "which would bring no triumphs"; a triumph, which was an honor coveted by all Republican generals, could be earned only by a victory over a foreign enemy; see also 1.121.

13-14 Understand as *quantum terrae pelagique parari potuit hoc sanguine quem dextrae ciuiles hauserunt.*

13   **quantum** the subject of *potuit*, followed by partitive gen.

14   **ciuiles . . . dextrae** i.e., the sword-hands of citizens

15-18   Lucan indicates the possible extent of Roman conquests, re-
ferring to east, west, south, and north in turn by means of
periphrases.

15   **Titan** a poetic designation for the sun

16   **quaque** i.e., *qua* ("where") + *-que*

      dies medius i.e., midday

17   **bruma** qualified by *rigens* and *nescia uere remitti*

      remitti pres. pass. infinitive after *nescia*

18   **Pontum** the Black Sea

19   **sub iuga** i.e., under Roman rule

      Seres a people imagined in the south of Africa but later identi-
fied with the Chinese

      isset plpf. subjunctive of *eo*, expressing the apodosis of an un-
real condition, i.e., if Rome had not become embroiled in civil
warfare; the verb has three subjects, *Seres* (pl.), *Araxes* (sing.)
and *gens* (sing.).

      Araxes a river in Armenia

      nascenti . . . Nilo dat., after *conscia*; lit. "the Nile being born,"
translate "the Nile's birth"; the Romans were fascinated by the
topic of the source of the Nile and Lucan includes a discussion
of the subject in Book 10.

21-23   Lucan addresses *Roma* directly, a second case of apostrophe.

21   **tum** i.e., then and only then

      si . . . supply *est* in the usual Latin expression for possession,
"if you have such a great . . ."

      nefandi echoes *nefas* (6)

22   **Latias** see n. on 1.9

      miseris fut. pf. of *mitto*

      tibi dat. after *defuit*, of the person experiencing the lack

      hostis i.e., an external enemy

24-31   A long sentence that starts with clauses introduced by *quod*, "the fact that," in anticipation of *non . . . auctor . . . erit*, "the originator . . . will not be . . . ." In the *quod* clauses Lucan (falsely) depicts the towns and lands of Italy as ruined and deserted because of the civil wars.

25   **urbibus Italiae** abl. of place where

        lapsis . . . muris abl. absolute

26   **domus** nom. pl., subject of *tenentur*

27   **rarus et** *et* is postponed; *rarus* qualifies *habitator*.

28   **horrida . . . inarata** both f. nom. sing., describing *Hesperia*

        quod parallel to *quod* at 24: see above

        dumis abl. after *horrida*

29   **Hesperia** lit. "the western land" (from a Greek perspective), usually denoting Italy, as here.

        manus a good example of the economy of Latin; technically the noun is nom. pl., subject of *desunt*, but it also functions as acc. pl., object of *poscentibus*.

        poscentibus aruis "the fields demand" hands to cultivate them.

30   Lucan attributes the deserted state of Italy not to her two enemies most renowned in history, Pyrrhus and Hannibal, but to herself.

        Pyrrhe ferox a momentary apostrophe of Pyrrhus, king of Epirus, who inflicted several major defeats on Rome during the third century BCE.

        auctor usually + gen., here + dat.

31   **Poenus** "the Carthaginian" is Hannibal, who waged the Second Punic War against Rome, 218–201 BCE; the adjective, used as a noun, is enough to identify him.

31-32   **nulli . . . ferro | contigit** impersonal verb + dat., lit. "it has befallen no sword"; for *ferrum*, see 1.8.

32   **alta sedent** "sink deep," *alta* in apposition to *uulnera*, almost adverbial in sense

ciuilis . . . dextrae gen. sing. after *uulnera*, i.e., "the wounds inflicted by a citizen's sword-hand"; Lucan repeats the phrase from 1.14.

33   **quod si** "but if," followed by three parallel clauses

uenturo . . . Neroni lit. "for Nero about to come," translated most easily as a noun, "for the coming of Nero"

fata n. pl., as often; a central concept in the poem, which has no conventional anthropomorphic deities; in their place Lucan deploys "fate" and "fortune" as agents in the plot, which seem at times to be personified as Fate and Fortune. "Fate" denotes the inevitable predetermined sequence of events while "Fortune" denotes the apparently random changes that can happen in life (see 1.84). Stoicism advocated psychological self-sufficiency in order to ignore the vagaries of fortune and to accept whatever fate has in store. Lucan has taken both concepts from Stoic philosophy, which enjoyed prominence among the Roman elite during the early empire; Lucan's uncle Seneca the Younger was instrumental in articulating the tenets of Stoicism in Latin.

34   **inuenere** for *inuenerunt*, 3rd person pl. pf. act. indicative

magno "for a lot," "at great cost," abl. of price

parantur here "are purchased"

35   **deis** abl. of agent; Lucan more or less identifies his vague "gods" with "fate" here; his treatment of the gods contrasts significantly with that of earlier Greek and Latin epic.

35-36   Understand as [*si*] *caelum suo Tonanti seruire potuit non nisi post bella gigantum saeuorum.*

suo . . . Tonanti "its own Thunderer": Lucan here equates Nero's power on earth with that of Jupiter (the Thunderer)'s power in heaven; for *Tonans*, cf. 1.196.

bella gigantum the giants challenged the authority of Jupiter and the other Olympian gods but the gods overcame them at the battle of Phlegra; this is often referred to as the gigantomachia.

37   **nihil** with adverbial force, i.e., we do not complain at all

scelera ipsa nefasque the subjects of *placent*

hac mercede abl. of price

placent supply *nobis*

38-45   This long sentence, addressed to Nero (*Caesar* 41), consists of four concessive clauses with subjunctive verbs expressing the idea of "although," to which the *tamen* clause replies. Lucan here specifies some of the most infamous events of the civil wars (both those between Caesar and the Pompeians and the wars that followed his assassination, between Mark Antony and Octavian, Caesar's heir) then caps the sentence by claiming that Nero's succession as emperor justifies all that carnage. Some scholars have thought that Lucan cannot be serious in this assertion; however, this form of flattery is common under autocratic regimes and more repulsive examples can be found from Roman and other societies. Without knowing his intentions, it seems more prudent to take Lucan at face value and to remember that great optimism accompanied Nero's accession to power at the age of 17 in 54 CE.

38   **diros . . . campos** Pharsalia's "plains" are "dreadful" because of the carnage that will happen there at the battle of Pharsalia (9 August 48 BCE).

Pharsalia a district in Thessaly near the town of Pharsalus; the chief battle between Caesar and Pompey (described in Book 7) was fought there.

39   **Poeni . . . manes** "Carthaginian shades," probably specific, i.e., Hannibal's ghost, which Lucan imagines as awaiting revenge for his defeats at the hands of the Romans during the Second Punic War (218–201 BCE); this revenge is figured as the battle of Thapsus in 46 BCE which was fought in Africa not far from Carthage.

40   A perfect case of a "Golden Line"; as at 1.3, polished poetic form conflicts with ghastly content.

ultima . . . proelia the decisive "final battle" (pl. for sing., as often in poetry) of the civil war was fought at Munda in Spain (17 March 45 BCE).

concurrant proelia *proelia* as the subject of the verb *concurro* is a poeticism.

41-42 **his . . . fatis** *fata* is here used in a different, weaker, sense from line 33; "to these deaths," almost "to these horrors."

Caesar i.e., Nero; Caesar became a *cognomen* of all the emperors and could be used alone to denote the reigning emperor, as here.

Perusina fames i.e., the long siege of Mark Antony's brother Lucius in Perusia (mod. Perugia) by Octavian all through the autumn and into the winter of 41 BCE.

Mutinae . . . labores another lengthy siege: Mark Antony besieged Decimus Brutus in Mutina (mod. Modena) 44–43 BCE.

42-43 Lucan supplies two further subjects of *accedant*, "although there be added . . ."; understand as *eae classes quas Leucas aspera premit* as well as the more straightforward *bella seruilia*.

quas premit aspera classes | Leucas "the fleets which rugged Leucas overwhelms" refers to the battle of Actium in 31 BCE, which was fought near the island of Leucas off the coast of western Greece; at this battle Octavian defeated Mark Antony and Cleopatra and thus established his supremacy.

seruilia bella "the slave wars" is a pejorative way of referring to the defeat of Pompey's son Sextus in the Sicilian seas in 36 BCE; Sextus' fleet was partly manned by slaves.

ardenti . . . Aetna the volcano on Sicily

44 **ciuilibus armis** "to citizens' weapons," i.e., weapons taken up in civil warfare

45 **tibi** gains emphasis from position: "because it was for you that everything was done."

∿ *The causes of the civil war, 1.67–157*

After further praise of Nero and anticipation of his deification, Lucan proceeds to analyse the various causes of the civil war, including (a) the fated and inevitable collapse of mighty structures, such as Rome (70–82); (b) the impossibility of power-sharing at Rome

(82–97); (c) the death of Crassus, the millionaire who was the third member of the so-called triumvirate (98–111); (d) the death of Julia, Caesar's daughter, who was married to Pompey to cement their political alliance (111–20); (e) the personalities of the two leaders, in which Pompey is compared to a massive old oak tree and Caesar is compared to a lightning-bolt (120–57).

68   **aperitur opus** "the task" that is "opened up" is actually the consequence of Lucan's mind prompting him to explain the causes, although the clauses are paratactic (i.e., parallel); accordingly, he devotes the next hundred lines or so to the causes of the civil war. Lucan's exploration of the causes serves at least two purposes: it allows him to establish certain themes which will recur throughout the poem and it allows him to postpone the narrative of the events he finds so horrifying, thus breaking with the Virgilian model of rapid narrative in order to make moral and aesthetic points.

68-69   **quid . . . quid . . .** both mark indirect questions dependent on an unexpressed verb such as *dicere*.

in arma i.e., "to war"

furentem again, civil war is described as a madness; cf. *furor* (1.8).

69   **orbi** dat. of disadvantage

70-72   There is no verb expressed, just four phrases in the nom. case (*series*, *negatum*, *lapsus*, and *Roma*); add "It was" to introduce these explanations of the civil war.

inuida fatorum series expresses the Greek idea of *nemesis*, i.e., that any form of overreaching (the Greek concept of *hybris*) is ultimately brought low; for *fatorum* see 1.33; the "chain of destiny" refers to the Stoic view of predetermination.

summis . . . negatum | stare diu lit. "the fact of it having been denied to the highest things to stand for a long time," i.e., "the impossibility of the highest lasting long"; *summis* is dat. pl. after *negatum*, which is n. sing. nom. of the pf. pass. participle used substantivally, as *certatum* (5).

nec se Roma ferens i.e., "Rome's inability to bear herself"

72-80   Lucan compares the collapse of Rome to the collapse of the universe. His picture of reversion to "primeval chaos" resembles the Stoic idea of the cycle of recurring universal conflagration. This long sentence consists of a temporal clause (*cum . . . chaos*) followed by six predictions (in the future tense), all of which represent disruptions of nature.

72   **conpage soluta** abl. absolute, referring to the "structure" of the universe (*mundus*)

73   **tot** goes with *saecula*, "so many ages"

        coegerit unusual sense; lit. "driven together" in the sense of "compressed" or "collapsed"

77   **fratri contraria Phoebe** highly poetic; Phoebe is the moon, the sister of Phoebus, the sun; Lucan imagines the moon "confronting" the sun, wanting to take over the daytime.

78   **bigas** the moon's chariot was imagined as a two-horse chariot, but the sun's as a four-horse chariot.

        agitare infinitive after *indignata*

79-80   "The whole discordant mechanism of the torn-apart universe will disrupt its own laws"; *discors* and *diuolsi* and *turbabit* emphasize the idea of disruption; it is typical of Lucan to reiterate his ideas like this.

81   **in se magna ruunt** the vague *magna* ("big things") is the subject of *ruunt*; another typical feature of Lucan's Latin: the short sentence full of impact; these are often called *sententiae* if they are generalizations, as here.

        laetis . . . rebus dat., "to prosperous things," so "to prosperity"

        hunc with *modum*

        numina another vague reference to the gods, like *deis* at 1.35

82   **crescendi** gerund after *modum*, "limit to growing"

        posuere for *posuerunt*, 3rd person pl. pf. act. indicative

        nec gentibus ullis i.e., not to any foreign race; Lucan echoes ideas expressed earlier, at 30–32.

83   **in** "against"

      terrae pelagique gen. after *potentem*; the reference to "land and sea," though conventional, reminds the reader of the huge extent of Roman power.

84   **inuidiam** Lucan echoes 1.70 *inuida fatorum series*

      Fortunam "chance" is here personified in the closest manner that Lucan ever gets to the anthropomorphic deities familiar from earlier epic; see 1.33. Fortune, who is prominent in Stoic philosophy, is a fickle and capricious power who can bestow success and failure on any individual; similar is the idea of the wheel of fortune, a powerful element in Roman thought.

84-85 **tu . . . Roma** a brief apostrophe to Rome, to drive home the contrast with foreign races: Rome is "the cause of [her own] troubles."

85   **facta . . . communis** a true pf. participle, "once Rome had become shared"

      tribus dominis dat. after *communis*; the "three masters" is another reference to the pact between Pompey, Caesar, and Crassus known as the first triumvirate (see 1.4); significantly, *dominus* is the word used to denote the master of a slave.

85-86 Lucan elaborates with a second clause; understand as *foedera feralia regni numquam missi* [agrees with *regni*] *in turbam*, "the ill-omened pact of tyranny, never shared among a crowd" (lit. "sent into a crowd"); *foedera* is pl. for sing. as often; on the negative tone of *regni*, see 1.4.

87-89 Now Lucan addresses the three "triumvirs" reproachfully.

87   **male concordes** "evilly in unison" or "harmonious in evil," i.e., working together with an outcome that is bad (for Rome).

88   **quid . . . iuuat?** supply *uos*, "why it is pleasing to [you]?"

89   **in medio** "in common"

89-93 Lucan strongly asserts the impossibility of sharing power by reference to unchanging natural phenomena, disposed in pairs, relating to earth + sea, then air + earth, then day + night.

89-91 **dum . . . leuabit . . . uoluent . . . sequetur** translate as if pres. tense: "as long as earth supports . . ."; *leuabit* has two subjects, *terra* and *aer.*

90 **uoluent Titana labores** lit. "his toils make Titan revolve"; *Titan* = the sun, as 1.15.

91 **caelo** abl. of place where

totidem per signa i.e., the twelve signs of the zodiac

92 **nulla fides** supply *erit*, "there will be no loyalty"

regni gen. after *sociis*, "associates in tyranny"

93 **consortis** gen. after *inpatiens*

gentibus ullis i.e., foreign races, as at 1.82

94 **credite** it is not clear who is the subject of the imperative; perhaps still the triumvirs, perhaps vaguer.

nec longe "not from afar," i.e., from Rome's own history

exempla the Romans learned all important moral lessons, positive and negative, from *exempla*, stories of role models drawn from history.

95 Another "Golden Line"; see 1.3. Lucan's choice to describe thus the primal act of fratricide at the founding of Rome conveys much about his attitude: he sets out to overturn the conventions of epic through shock tactics.

fraterno . . . sanguine Romulus is said to have killed Remus in a quarrel over the new city-walls of Rome. For Lucan, this act of fratricide is a predictor of the civil warfare of his poem.

96 **pretium** in apposition to the subjects, *tellus pontusque*

tanti . . . furoris reprises 1.8, 68

97 **exiguum dominos commisit asylum** lit. "the tiny asylum brought its masters to fight (one another)"; the point is that the stakes were minuscule compared with those of the civil war and yet the two brothers fought to the death. The asylum was the sanctuary for slaves and criminals established by Romulus, from which Rome grew.

98   **temporis angusti . . . concordia** gen. of quality, "concord [consisting] of a narrow time"

        concordia discors a paradox, a literary technique relished by Lucan

99   **ducum** gen. pl. of *dux*, after *sponte*, lit. "by the will of the leaders"; Lucan calls both his main protagonists, Pompey and Caesar, *duces.*

99-100 Understand as *mora sola belli futuri erat Crassus medius* ("in between"). Crassus was the fabulously wealthy member of the so-called first triumvirate and had played a delicate political balancing act of support for Pompey and Caesar. Lucan here introduces an idea central to his poem, that of "delay." In sharp contrast with Virgil, and Homer before him, Lucan does not launch into the action but instead delays initiating his narrative of the civil war. His own poetic concern with delay is matched by his attention to instances of delay within the narrative.

100-106 The first simile of the poem—an elaborate one, comparing Crassus with the isthmus of Corinth, the thin strip of land connecting the Peloponnese with mainland Greece and separating the Ionian Sea to the west from the Aegean Sea to the east. Lucan's focus is negative, on the turmoil unleashed by the removal of the isthmus and by the death of Crassus. In this way human activities are likened to a natural disaster.

101   **Isthmos** the subject (Greek form of nom.) of *frangat*, modified by the adjective *gracilis* and the rel. clause *qui secat et . . . separat . . . nec patitur*

103   **Aegaeo** supply *mari*; either abl. or dat., "smash by means of the Aegean" or "smash against the Aegean"

103-4   **saeua | arma ducum dirimens** a true pres. participle: "at the time when he was keeping apart the leaders' savage weapons"

104   **miserando funere** goes with *maculauit*, denoting the attendant circumstances, "in lamentable death"

105   Not a perfect "Golden Line" (see 1.3) but nevertheless elegantly balanced through chiasmus.

Assyrias . . . Carrhas Carrhae, an important city in the Assyrian empire (mod, Herran), was where the Parthians defeated and killed Crassus in 53 BCE.

Latio . . . sanguine also with *maculauit*, abl. of means

106 A true "Golden Line" (see 1.3); as often, Lucan seems to reserve this poetic effect for especially grim material.

Romanos . . . furores the civil war is again labeled madness by Lucan; cf. 1.8, 68, 96

damna subject of *soluerunt*; the "losses" or "disasters" are envisaged from the Roman perspective, with *Parthica* meaning not "of the Parthians" but in effect "to the Parthians" or "inflicted by the Parthians"

107-8 A brief apostrophe to the Parthians, here called "sons of Arsaces," after Arsaces, the first king of the Parthian dynasty.

plus subject of *actum est*

uobis abl. of agency with *actum est*

bellum uictis civile dedistis a condensed and surprising, almost paradoxical, statement (cf. 1.81); whatever victors (the Parthians) might give to "the defeated" (the Romans), one would not expect it to be civil war.

109 **diuiditur** pres. for pf., as often in epic narrative

regnum on the word's negative implications see 1.4; cf. 1.86

populi . . . potentis gen., after *fortuna*

110 The three rel. clauses anticipate their subject, *fortuna*, in the next line; all three use the verb *possidet*.

totum . . . orbem another grand claim for the extent of Roman power

111 **non cepit . . . duos** i.e., Pompey and Caesar; for *capio* = "to contain" or "to be big enough for," think of our word "capacious."

111-14 Julia, the daughter of Julius Caesar, was another obstacle to strife between Pompey and Caesar: in 59 BCE she married Pompey as part of the political allegiance between the two men, but she died in childbirth in 54 BCE.

112   **diro ferales omine** as often in post-Augustan Latin, an adjective can govern another phrase; Lucan probably means that the end of the marriage was a grim omen of the breakdown of the relationship between father-in-law and son-in-law.

        taedas by mentioning the "wedding-torches" Lucan makes it appear that Pompey's marriage to Julia was briefer than it was; to call "wedding-torches" "deadly" (*ferales*) sounds paradoxical.

113   **Parcarum** the three Fates, Clotho, Lachesis, and Atropos, who were imagined to spin, measure, and cut off human lives as if they were threads; cf. 3.18–19.

113-14 **saeua . . . manu** with *Parcarum*

114   **intercepta** nom., of Julia

        quod si "but if"

115   **in luce** i.e., alive

        moras pl. for sing.

        furentem goes with both *uirum* and *parentem*; Lucan again emphasizes the madness of civil war, cf. 1.68.

117   **excusso . . . ferro** abl. absolute; in English it works better to turn it around and make it a main verb parallel to the finite verb: here "you alone could have . . . thrown away their swords and joined their armed hands," rather than "the sword having been thrown away"; *ferro* is sing. for pl.

118   **ut** introduces a simile which represents Julia as the Sabine women; according to early Roman legend, the Sabine women were carried off by Romulus and Romans, who needed wives, and when their fathers came to fight for their return they reconciled their husbands with their fathers.

        generos soceris the juxtaposition represents what the Sabine women are able to achieve; *soceris* is dat. after *iunxere*

        mediae some Latin adjectives, including *medius*, resist being rendered as adjectives in English; the sense is adverbial, "in between."

        iunxere for *iunxerunt*, 3rd person pl. pf. act. indicative

119-20   A brief apostrophe to Julia.

119   **discussa** supply *est*

         bellum mouere a standard Latin idiom, "to initiate war"

120   **permissum** supply *est*, followed by the infinitive *mouere*

         ducibus dat. after the impersonal pass. *permissum*

         stimulos dedit aemula uirtus lit. "rivalrous excellence gave
         them the spurs," so "rivalry in excellence spurred them on";
         although *uirtus* looks like English "virtue," that is hardly ever
         the best translation, because it has acquired irrelevant Chris-
         tian overtones since antiquity; it helps to remember that the
         root of *uirtus* is *uir* and that the abstract noun is the quality of
         being a [proper] man.

121-24   Lucan introduces his two protagonists, Pompey and Caesar,
         addressing a brief apostrophe to each (*tu . . . Magne . . . ; te . . .*).

121-23   Pompey's rivalry is rooted in fear that Caesar's more recent
         achievements will eclipse his own. Pompey had celebrated
         three triumphs, over Numidia (81 BCE), Spain (71 BCE), and
         Asia (62 BCE), and in 67 BCE had overcome the pirates, who
         had been plaguing shipping throughout the Mediterranean;
         Caesar's conquest of Gaul was more recent than any of these
         achievements (58–51 BCE), though he did not celebrate his tri-
         umph over Gaul until 46 BCE.

121   Another "Golden Line" (see 1.3), with striking juxtaposition
         of *noua* and *ueteres.*

         ne . . . obscurent . . . et . . . cedat clauses of fearing after *times*

         triumphos a triumph was a spectacular celebratory proces-
         sion of a victorious Roman general from the Campus Mar-
         tius outside the walls through the city to the temple of Jupiter
         Capitolinus on the Capitoline Hill; the criteria for the award
         of a triumph were stringent (see 1.12) and relatively few were
         granted

122   **uictis . . . Gallis** Caesar's conquest of Gaul during the 50s BCE
         is memorialized in his own account, his *Commentaries*, which
         we call the Gallic Wars.

piratica laurea a triumphing general was awarded a crown of laurel; Lucan's expression here is compact: i.e., the laurel crown awarded for victory over the pirates.

123 **Magne** "the Great," the *cognomen* (something like "nickname") given to Pompey early in his career, in 81 BCE, after victories in Sicily and Africa; Lucan usually prefers to call him *Magnus* rather than *Pompeius* (more than twice as often).

series ususque both nom. sing., with *erigit*

123-24 Lucan associates Caesar's rivalry with his endurance of difficult tasks and his ambition; the fighting in Gaul in the late 50s had been especially challenging. By 50 BCE Caesar was seeking the consulship again, after Pompey's sole consulship in 52 BCE.

124 **inpatiens . . . loci . . . secundi** another case where an adjective governs its phrase; *inpatiens* takes the gen. of the thing not tolerated.

fortuna another subject of *erigit*; refers to Caesar's own "fortune"; Fortune personified presides over Caesar's rise—that is why he swears allegiance to her as he crosses the Rubicon (1.225–27) and commits himself into her hands as he ventures a dangerous sea-crossing in Book 5 (5.510 and 696–97).

125-26 The comparison modulates from the 2nd into the 3rd person.

nec quemquam "and not anyone" (acc.); the phrase goes with *priorem* (in the case of Caesar) and *parem* (in the case of Pompey); in other words, Lucan asserts that Caesar was prepared to share the top position but that Pompey was not—one of the most negative things he says about Pompey.

iam ferre potest goes with each of *Caesar* and *Pompeius*

Pompeius Lucan generally calls him *Magnus* (as 1.123).

126-28 Lucan weighs the two sides in terms of justification and authority. Although he declines to pass explicit judgement, saying that it is forbidden knowledge (*scire nefas*), it is clear here and throughout that his sympathies are with Pompey.

127 **scire nefas** supply *est*; lit. "[it is] a crime to know"; *nefas* is a favorite word (already used at 1.6 and 37).

magno se iudice quisque tuetur lit. "each protects himself with a great judge," where "judge" means authority or umpire; Lucan immediately explains who these judges are: the gods are on Caesar's side (hence the establishment of the principate) but Cato is on Pompey's side.

128 This line is shaped by the contrast between *uictrix* and *uicta*, both agreeing with *causa*; the effect is to suggest that Cato alone is almost equivalent to "the gods." Marcus Porcius Cato is the third major protagonist of the poem and the "hero" of Book 9, when he assumes leadership of the Republican armies after Pompey's assassination. He was famously a model of stern virtue and austere Stoicism.

129 **nec coiere pares** *coiere* is for *coierunt*, 3rd person pl. pf. act. indicative; take *nec* with *pares*: "and they came together not equally matched." This brief sentence introduces an extended description of the two protagonists; Lucan starts each description directly and provides a telling simile (129–57).

129-43 Lucan starts with Pompey, referring to him only as *alter*, "one [of two]."

uergentibus annis abl. absolute

130 **in senium** a misrepresentation by Lucan, as Pompey was only six years older than Caesar.

togae after *longo . . . usu*; the toga, the characteristic garb of the Roman citizen (as opposed to the Roman soldier), metaphorically denotes "peace-time," as at 9.199; Pompey's previous experience of active warfare had been fourteen years earlier, in his victory over King Mithridates of Pontus in 63 BCE.

131 **ducem** i.e., leadership; Lucan strains the language a little here.

famae . . . petitor it is central to Lucan's portrayal of Pompey that he craves popularity.

132 **multa dare in uulgus** "was generous to the crowd"; Pompey staged shows and games to entertain the people, e.g., at the opening of his theater (Plutarch, *Pompey* 52).

dare initiates a sequence of five historic infinitives, in place of the pf. indicative; cf. 147–49 below.

totus best translated as an adverb, "totally"

popularibus auris another metaphor, i.e., the "breezes" of favor, popularity

133   **inpelli** pres. pass. infinitive

sui . . . theatri Pompey built Rome's first permanent, stone theater in 55 BCE.

134   **nouas** the adjective almost has adverbial force, "anew."

134-35   **priori . . . fortunae** Lucan characterizes Pompey as relying on his former achievements and looking back to the past.

135   **stat magni nominis umbra** "he stands, the shadow of a great name"; the phrase *magni nominis* plays on Pompey's *cognomen* (see 1.123) Magnus

136-43   An extended simile, comparing Pompey to a great oak tree, impressive and still venerated alone but liable to be toppled by the first strong wind; it is important that the tree is ancient and static.

136   **quercus** governs *sublimis, gestans, haerens* and *fixa est*; *effundens* and *efficit*; *casura*; and *sola . . . colitur.*

137   **exuuias ueteres populi** i.e., armor stripped from enemies in former battles and hung on the tree by the people as dedications, a standard practice in antiquity.

138   **dona ducum** i.e., the dedications made by generals too

nec iam ualidis take together, "not now strong"

139   **aera** acc. sing. (Greek form), three syllables

140   **trunco non frondibus** i.e., although the tree has no foliage (hence *nudos . . . ramos*, 139) its sheer bulk is enough to create shade.

141   **quamuis** governs both subjunctives, *nutet* and *tollant*

casura fut. participle, "about to fall" or "ready to fall"

142   **siluae** nom. pl., meaning "trees"; the "trees that raise them-
        selves all around with sturdy trunks" are younger competitors
        for power who still cannot diminish Pompey's authority.

143   **colitur** the worship of the oak tree matches the veneration of
        Pompey.

143-57 Lucan now describes Caesar.

143-44 **non . . . tantum . . . erat** "there was . . . not only . . ."

144   **nomen, fama** both nom., with *ducis*; Caesar's military achieve-
        ments, in Asia and Spain and most recently Gaul, were on an
        unprecedented scale.

144-45 **nescia uirtus | stare loco** lit. "excellence that does not know
        how to stand in [one] place"

145   **solus . . . pudor** supply *est*

        non uincere bello in apposition to *solus . . . pudor*; this prob-
        ably means "to conquer not with war," i.e., without war; Lucan
        represents Caesar's delight in waging war.

146   **quo spes quoque ira uocasset** two parallel phrases introduced
        by *quo* ("to where") after *ferre manum*; *spes* and *ira* are both
        subjects of *uocasset* (for *uocauisset*).

147   **ferre manum** the first of four historic infinitives, in place of
        pf. indicative; cf. 132–35; "to carry one's hand" is to move into
        action.

        parcere with *numquam*, followed by dat. *ferro*

        temerando gerundive, lit. "that had to be defiled," i.e., Caesar
        "never flinched from defiling his sword."

148   **fauori** dat. after *insto*; Lucan represents Caesar as so confi-
        dent in divine favor that he can insist on it.

149   **numinis** Lucan does not specify the deity but leaves it vague,
        "of divinity."

149-50 **inpellens . . . gaudens** the pres. participles convey a sense of
        dynamism through their simultaneity with the main verbs:
        Caesar is all action.

quidquid sibi summa petenti | obstaret translate "all obstacles to his high ambitions"; *quidquid* is object of *inpellens* and subject of *obstaret*; *sibi* is dat. after *obsto*; *petenti* is dat. with *sibi*; *summa* is the n. pl. object of *petenti*, lit. "the highest things."

151-57   an extended simile, comparing Caesar to a thunderbolt which causes terror and devastation along its irresistible path; crucial is the thunderbolt's energy and movement; the clear implication is that the unstoppable power of the thunderbolt will shatter and fell the giant oak tree.

151   **expressum** pf. pass. participle agreeing with *fulmen*

uentis abl. of cause after *expressum*

152   This line describes the sounds made by the thunderbolt, *sonitu* and *fragore.*

inpulsi pf. pass. participle of *inpello*; technically belongs with *aetheris* but perhaps describes *mundi* too.

155   **in sua templa furit** "it rages against its own precincts," the notion of mad rage yet again; the action of the thunderbolt symbolizes Caesar's waging war on fellow Romans.

155-56   **nulla . . . exire uetante | materia** abl. absolute, *exire* infinitive after *uetante*

156   **magnam . . . magnam** the repetition gives huge emphasis to the destruction (*stragem*) caused by the thunderbolt and may also be a play on Pompey's name *Magnus.*

cadens, **reuertens** pres. participles of action simultaneous with the verb *dat*, "as it falls" and "as it returns"

∾ *Caesar at the Rubicon, 1.183–227*

After all these preliminaries about the causes of the civil war, Lucan finally embarks on his narrative. Caesar advances to the river Rubicon but is immediately halted on the banks by a vision of the city of Rome, personified, in mourning. In response to her words Caesar uncharacteristically hesitates, utters a prayer to the gods of Rome in self-justification, then crosses the river. The narrative of action is outweighed by a long simile in which Caesar is compared to an African lion. Lucan then describes the Rubicon and the crossing of Caesar's troops made easy by his strategic skill. The momentous significance of his act is marked by another, shorter, speech from Caesar. The contrast with usual epic narrative technique is strong; Lucan deploys delay and narrative doubling to avoid broaching the horrendous topic of the civil war.

183   In a single line Lucan gets Caesar over the Alps, an arduous journey, especially in winter (hence *gelidas*); by contrast, Livy had devoted a substantial part of Book 21 of his history of the Roman Republic to Hannibal's crossing of the Alps. Lucan's choice of the verb *supero* suggests that Caesar has "defeated" the Alps as well as "crossed" them.

184-85 **animo . . . ceperat** "in his mind he had conceived"

185   **uentum est** impersonal pass., lit. "there was a coming"

      Rubiconis a small river in north Italy flowing into the Adriatic Sea not far from Ariminum (mod. Rimini), which formed the boundary between the province of Gallia Cisalpina and Italy.

186   **uisa** supply *est*, pf. pass. with *adstare* and *loqui*, "seemed" or "appeared"

      duci dat. after *uisa* [*est*], "to the leader," i.e., Caesar

      patriae trepidantis imago Lucan deploys visions and dreams very sparingly in his epic; Caesar's vision of Rome is balanced by the appearance of the ghost of Julia to Pompey at the start of Book 3; after that, there are no further dreams until Book 7, where Pompey has a dream before the battle of Pharsalia and Caesar and his men have nightmares afterwards.

187   **clara . . . obscuram** Lucan juxtaposes the contrasting terms.

      uultu after *maestissima*, "in her face"

188   Another "Golden Line" (see 1.3)

      turrigero . . . uertice in Roman art cities were often represented wearing turreted crowns; in the case of Rome, this may be modeled on the iconography of Cybele, the great

mother goddess from Phrygia whose cult was brought to
Rome around 200 BCE.

189   **caesarie** it is hard to resist seeing a play on Caesar's name here.

190   **permixta** n. pl. acc., perhaps with ellipse of *uerba*

191   **uiri** "men" as in "warriors" or "soldiers"

192   **si ciues** supply *uenitis*, i.e., "if you come as [Roman] citizens"

       huc usque licet supply *uobis uenire*; the reason it was illegal
       for Caesar to progress further is that as governor of Gallia
       Cisalpina he was permitted to deploy his army there, but in
       Italy (i.e., once he crossed the Rubicon) he was not.

192-94 Since Lucan's Caesar almost never experiences fear or appre-
       hension (as the rest of the poem reveals), his being overcome by
       "trembling," "weakness" (*languor*), and hesitation here marks
       the moment as profoundly significant; Lucan emphasizes the
       effect of Rome's words on Caesar by repeating the idea of his
       being halted (*gressum . . . coercens* and *tenuit uestigia*).

194   **in extrema . . . ripa** "on the edge of the bank"

195   **mox** indicates that Caesar "soon" recovers self-command.

195-203 In response, Caesar appeals to the gods of Rome to favor him. The
       gods he names—Jupiter Capitolinus, the Phrygian house-gods,
       Quirinus, Jupiter of Latium, Vesta, and Rome herself—combine
       the highest god, Jupiter, with evocations of Rome's foundation
       myths, including the myth of Julius Caesar's own ancestor Ae-
       neas. The effect is to emphasize Caesar's Romanness.

195-96 The word order is rather contorted; understand as *o [Iuppiter]
       Tonans, [tu] qui de rupe Tarpeia moenia urbis magnae prospicis.*

       Tarpeia de rupe a precipice on the Capitoline Hill in Rome,
       which was where the temple of Jupiter Capitolinus was located.

       Tonans the cult title of Jupiter Capitolinus, as at 1.35

196-97 **Phrygii . . . penates | gentis Iuleae** the household gods (*pena-
       tes*) brought from Troy (in Phrygia) to Italy by Aeneas, who was
       the father of Iulus (also called Ascanius) who was claimed as
       ancestor of the Julian clan and hence of Julius Caesar himself.

197 **rapti secreta Quirini** the cult of Quirinus, a god worshipped on the Quirinal Hill at Rome and usually identified with Romulus, the founder of Rome, after he was "carried off" (*rapti*) to heaven and deified.

198 Jupiter of Latium was worshipped in an ancient cult at a temple on the Alban Mount in Latium; since the settlement of Alba Longa was said to have been founded by Aeneas' son Iulus and since Rome was said to have been founded from Alba Longa, Caesar is again linking himself with the early history of Rome.

199 **Vestales . . . foci** pl. for sing.; the Vestal Virgins tended the sacred fire supposedly brought from Troy by Aeneas, in the temple of Vesta in the heart of the Forum at Rome.

summi . . . numinis gen. after *instar*

instar often follows the word(s) that it governs.

200 **Roma** Caesar makes the goddess the climax of his catalogue of divine powers, with a compliment to her, and addresses his prayer to her alone (*faue*, sing.). Pompey uses exactly the same words, *Roma, faue coeptis*, at 8.322 when out of desperation he proposes an alliance with the Parthians, another act of disloyalty.

coeptis dat. after *faue*

201 **terraque marique** the phrase *terra marique* ("by land and sea") is standard; here the extra -*que* elevates the tone, as fits a prayer.

202 **liceat modo** lit. "let it only be permitted," i.e., "if I am permitted"; his words echo Rome's words, *huc usque licet* (192). Caesar is claiming loyalty to Rome and legitimacy for entering Italy under arms; for the legal situation, see Introduction.

203 **ille erit ille** the repetition elevates the tone and conveys Caesar's passion.

nocens i.e., "guilty" of causing civil war; cf. 1.126–27 where Lucan poses the question "who more justly took up weapons?"

qui me tibi fecerit hostem he implies Pompey, as the leader of the senatorial cause.

fecerit fut. pf.

204   **moras soluit belli** whereas Lucan seems anxious to delay his account of the civil war, his protagonist Caesar is keen to initiate the action.

205   **signa** the standards lead the way; the rest of the army crosses after Lucan has inserted a simile.

205-12   Another extended simile: Caesar is compared with a lion goading himself to fight and persisting in his attack even when he is wounded; Lucan thus implies that Caesar is likewise goading himself into a rage.

206   **Libyes** gen. sing. (Greek form); Lucan specifies his lion as "Libyan" to invite the Roman reader to draw a comparison between Caesar and Rome's "Libyan" enemy, Hannibal.

uiso . . . hoste abl. absolute

208   **mox** Lucan repeats the sequence of hesitation and quick recovery from Caesar's encounter with Rome (192–95, NB *mox* 195); *mox* is followed by two subordinate clauses introduced by *ubi* and *si*; the main verb is *exit* (212).

saeuae . . . uerbere caudae "with his fiercely lashing tail"

209   **murmur** cognate acc. after *infremuit*, unusual diction

210   **torta** pf. pass. participle of *torqueo*, with *lancea*, i.e., "once hurled"

leuis gen. sing. with *Mauri*

212   **per ferrum . . . exit** a strange expression, lit. "he goes out through the weapon," i.e., he runs onto the weapon and drives it deeper into himself.

tanti . . . uulneris gen. after *securus*

213-19   A description of the river Rubicon, setting the scene for the crossing by Caesar's troops in January 49 BCE.

214   **puniceus** a gloss on the "red" element in the name *Rubic*on

215-16   **certus | limes** in apposition to *Rubicon*, "as a fixed boundary"

217   **auxerat** the subject is *Cynthia* (218) and also *Alpes* (219).

218   **tertia iam grauido pluuialis Cynthia cornu** condensed po-
       etic language: i.e., it had already been raining steadily. *Cyn-
       thia* denotes Diana and hence the moon (counterpart to her
       brother Apollo as the sun); *tertia Cynthia* is the third night
       of the new moon and her "laden crescent" is a meteorological
       effect associated with rain.

219   **madidis Euri resolutae flatibus Alpes** more poetic language:
       lit. "the Alps unfastened by the wet blasts of the Eurus," i.e.,
       the Alpine snows melted by a moist wind from the east.

220   **primus** technically an adjective but adverbial in sense, espe-
       cially in the nom. case.

       sonipes a poetic word for a horse; collective sing., i.e., the
       cavalry.

       in obliquum . . . amnem lit. "facing the slanting river," but it
       is the cavalry and not the river that is "aslant"; Caesar's strate-
       gy is to have the cavalry break the force of the water so that the
       rest of his army can cross safely, as Lucan explains (221–22).

221   **excepturus aquas** the fut. participle here denotes purpose.

221-22 **molli . . . uado** abl. of manner, "with an easy crossing"

222   **iam** with *fracti*

223   **superato gurgite** abl. absolute

224   **Hesperiae** i.e., Italy

       et postponed from the start of its clause; connects *constitit*
       with *attigit*.

225   **temerata . . . iura** Caesar's perspective was that his opponents
       had acted illegally against him by expelling the tribunes, who
       had fled to him for protection.

226   **te, Fortuna, sequor** emphatically "it is you, Fortune, that I
       follow"; Lucan has Caesar claim a special relationship with
       the goddess Fortuna.

       foedera presumably deals such as the "first triumvirate"

       sunto 3rd person pl. pres. imperative of *sum*

227   **his** i.e., *foedera*; this is the emendation printed by Housman

utendum est supply *mihi*; the gerund conveys necessity: "I must use."

iudice bello abl. after *utor*; *iudice* is in apposition to *bello*: "war as my referee"; this is Lucan's version of the famous statement attributed to Caesar, *alea iacta est* ("the die is cast"), meaning that he has made his decision and the outcome is out of his hands.

∾ *Rome is abandoned, 1.486–504*

At the word of Caesar's relentless advance through Italy, the people and the Senate abandon Rome as if it were on fire, imagining that northern invaders are right behind him, ready to sack Rome. The scene at Rome resembles a sacked city (a literary set-piece, or *topos*) and Lucan adds an extended simile of a shipwreck.

486-89   **nec solum uulgus . . . sed curia et ipse . . . patres** Lucan betrays his assumption that while the people might be prey to terror, the Roman senatorial elite should be expected to show intelligence and self-control; the defeat of this expectation shows how menacing Caesar seems to everyone.

486   **uulgus** often a dismissive or contemptuous word

     inani because the reports of northern invaders are without foundation

487   **curia** the senate-house, hence by metonymy the Senate itself

488   **patres** the senators, whose title was in full *patres conscripti*, "conscript fathers"

488-89   **inuisa . . . belli . . . decreta** "the dreaded declaration of war" (*decreta* is pl. for sing.) is Lucan's way of referring to the *senatus consultum ultimum*, which was the senate's declaration of a state of emergency and the award of emergency powers to the consuls and other magistrates against a public enemy; for Caesar's account see *Civil War* 1.5.

489   **fugiens** this pres. participle vividly depicts the senate voting on the emergency while actually running out of the senate-house.

490 **quae tuta petant et quae metuenda relinquant** indirect questions after *incerti*, agreeing with *patres* (the senators); *tuta* and *metuenda* are both n. pl. acc. objects of their respective verbs, lit. "what safe things they might seek and what fearful things they might abandon."

491 **quo quemque fugae tulit impetus** rel. clause; understand as *quo* [to where] *impetus fugae quemque tulit*; Lucan's wording makes the fleeing senators the passive prey of their emotions: they are running away without any forethought or plan.

491-92 **urguent | praecipitem populum** again, it is no surprise that the *populus* is fleeing "headlong" but for the senators to "press on their heels" is undignified.

492-93 The senators actually break through the long lines of ordinary people.

493-504 Lucan here adapts the standard description of the captured and sacked city, a *topos* in Greco-Roman works of history and epic. He does so to make an ironic, paradoxical point: that Rome has not been sacked.

493 **credas** the 2nd person verb draws the reader in with an invitation to envisage the scene; *credas* is followed by two acc. + infinitive phrases.

494 **iam quatiente ruina** "with collapse now shaking (them)"; as often, Lucan heaps up the central idea, here that of instability (*quatiente, ruina, nutantes,* and *pendere*)

495 **turba** its verb is *ruit* (498)

496-97 **rebus . . . adflictis** probably dat. with *spes unica*, "the sole salvation for their battered fortunes"; *res* (pl.) often = "situation."

497 **foret** equivalent of *esset*; the subjunctive indicates that this is what they are thinking.

patrios . . . muros Lucan's word-play, making the *patres conscripti* leave their *patrios . . . muros* ("ancestral walls"), is meant to be shocking.

498 **inconsulta** agrees with *turba*

498-503 Lucan develops a lengthy simile of a shipwreck to depict the flight from Rome, playing on the ancient metaphor of the "ship of state."

499 **Syrtibus** dangerous shallows and sandbanks off the coast of Africa between Cyrene and Carthage; Lucan envisages the South Wind driving back the water from the sandbanks and thus making the shallows even shallower and more dangerous.

500 Another "Golden Line" (see 1.3); lit. "the broken weight (pl. for sing.) of the sail-bearing mast resounded," i.e., as it crashed down.

501 **desilit** pres. for pf., for vividness

deserta puppe abl. absolute; best treated as a separate clause: "abandons ship and"

502 **nauita** second subject of *desilit*; collective sing., "the sailors" i.e., "the crew"

nondum sparsa conpage carinae another abl. absolute; "with the structure of the boat not yet broken up"

503 **naufragium sibi quisque facit** i.e., everyone anticipates the disaster.

Vrbe relicta another abl. absolute, again best treated as a separate clause, "they abandon Rome"

504 **in bellum fugitur** impersonal pass., lit. "there is a fleeing"; this is possibly Lucan's most brilliant paradox: the citizens of Rome think they are running away from Caesar but in fact they are "fleeing towards war."

∾ Pompey is visited by the ghost of Julia, 3.8–35

As Pompey sails away from Italy for the last time, his dead wife Julia appears to him in a dream in the shape of a Fury and vows to hound him forever (12–34). Pompey married Julia, who was Caesar's daughter, in 59 BCE to seal their political alliance, but she died in childbirth in 54 BCE. This brief episode provides an equivalent to

Caesar's vision of Roma as he is about to cross the Rubicon (1.185–
94). Lucan makes sparing use of dreams and visions; the only others
in the poem as it survives are in Book 7.

8   **cesserunt** + dat., *somno*, "yield to"

9   **ducis** "the leader," often used to refer to one of the protago-
nists, here Pompey.

10   **uisa** for *uisa est*, "seemed"

      Iulia either take *Iulia* as the subject and *imago* in apposition,
or the other way around.

11   **furialis** "like a fury"; the Furies were ancient powers who
avenged wrongs done to family members.

12   **sedibus Elysiis campoque . . . piorum** the parts of the Under-
world inhabited by the good

      expulsa pf. participle pass., of Julia

14   **post bellum ciuile** i.e., since the civil war began

14-15 Understand as *uidi ipsa Eumenidas tenentes lampadas quas
quaterent armis uestris*. The subjunctive *quaterent* expresses
purpose: "to brandish at your weapons." In Greek the Furies
were the Eumenides, whose name by irony means "Kindly
Ones." Firebrands were among their usual apparatus.

16-17 **Acherontis adusti | portitor** The "ferryman of scorched
Acheron" is Charon, who ferried the souls of the dead across
the rivers of the Underworld. The river Acheron is here called
"scorched" by association with another river, Phlegethon, lit.
"Fiery."

17   **Tartara** here n. pl. subject.; Tartarus was the part of the Un-
derworld where the wicked were punished, hence *in . . . po-
enas* = "for punishments."

18-19 The "sisters" are the three Fates (*Parcae*), Clotho, Lachesis,
and Atropos; cf. 1.113–14. Clotho's task was to spin the thread
of life, Lachesis' to measure it, and Atropos' to cut it. But here
Lucan has all three "breaking" the threads full-time, to indi-
cate the massive scale of slaughter.

operi . . . sufficiunt "are equal to the work"

20 **coniuge me** abl. absolute in the present tense, i.e., simultaneous with the main verb: "while I was your wife."

triumphos on the Roman triumph, see 1.12, 121; on Pompey's three triumphs, see 1.121–23.

21 **toris** "marriage-bed" stands for "marriage" or "wife"

21-23 Julia extrapolates from the fate of Cornelia's first husband, Crassus, who died at the battle of Carrhae fighting the Parthians in 53 BCE, to assert that Cornelia is bad luck for all her husbands.

semper probably with *detrahere in cladem*; possibly with *fato damnata*.

potentes with *maritos*

innupsit tepido . . . busto "married into a warm tomb," referring to the ashes from the cremation. Julia's claim is unfair: the usual ten-month period of mourning had been observed and Pompey married Cornelia two years after Julia's death.

paelex Cornelia The name is postponed to create a shocking oxymoron: Julia calls Cornelia, whose family was among the most eminent and who was Pompey's legal spouse, a "paramour" or "mistress."

25 **dum** "provided that," followed by three subjunctive verbs, *liceat, sit,* and *teneat*

non belongs not with the verb but with the adjective *securos*, i.e., "disturbed"

26 **uestro . . . amori** i.e., the love between Pompey and Cornelia

27 Julia plans to haunt Pompey's nights just as her father Caesar occupies Pompey's days.

28 **coniunx** By calling Pompey "husband" she indicates that she regards the marriage as continuing beyond her death.

obliuia n. pl. subject; translate as singular.

Lethaeae ripae Lethe was the river of forgetfulness in the Underworld.

29   **tui** gen. sing. of the pronoun *tu*, after *inmemorem*

30   **sequi** as often in Latin, *sequor* means "follow with a purpose," e.g., "chase" as here.

    te bella gerente abl. absolute, pres. tense, denoting simultaneous action: "while you are waging wars"

31-32   **numquam tibi . . . genero non esse licebit** lit. "It will never be permitted to you to not be a son-in-law," with *genero* matching the dat. case of *tibi*.

33   **tua pignora** the "pledges" made when he married Julia

33-34   **bellum | te faciet ciuile meum** "civil war will make you mine"

35   **dilapsa** as often, the past participle of a deponent verb has a vague temporal reference.

∾ *Caesar fells the sacred grove, 3.399–445*

As Caesar races from Rome towards Spain, crossing the Alps again (cf. 1.183), the only resistance he meets is from the city of Massilia. Caesar besieges the city, felling the forests round about to make his blockade. This passage pauses the action while Lucan describes the sacred grove that Caesar cuts down. First, he describes the grove in awe-inspiring terms (399–425), then he narrates how Caesar takes the initiative in felling the grove when his troops hesitate out of fear (426–45). Although it is clear that Caesar's troops needed wood, we can be confident that this episode is invented by Lucan to enhance his characterization of Caesar as a megalomaniac who has no fear of the gods or of committing sacrilege. His destruction of the grove enacts the implication of the pair of similes in Book 1, where Lucan suggests that the aged and venerated oak tree (Pompey) will be toppled by the powerful lightning-bolt (Caesar).

399-425   Descriptive passages such as this are standard in ancient epic poetry, providing an atmospheric setting for the following narration of the events that take place there; cf. Lucan's description of the setting of the witch Erichtho's necromantic rites starting at 6.642. Here Lucan marks off this section by starting and ending it with the word *lucus*.

A *lucus* was a sacred grove; this one is numinous in a sinister and terrifying way: it is a place of barbarous rites and primitive images; it belongs to no familiar deity but to an unnamed "master of the grove" (425). Lucan creates a paradox in the tension between the etymology of the word, connected with *lux* ("light") and *lucere* ("to shine"), and the darkness that characterizes this particular grove, to which he draws attention in the word that begins line 400, *obscurum*.

This sinister grove seems designed to contrast with an idealized landscape that recurs in classical poetry, the *locus amoenus* (lit. "pleasant place") so typical of pastoral poetry in particular. The characteristics of the *locus amoenus* include pleasant, cooling shade provided by spreading trees, moving water (a stream or spring), lush and fertile vegetation, soothing sounds (turtle-doves or bees), and potential for benign epiphany; the *locus amoenus* is often the setting for beautiful song. In contrast, Lucan has here created a *locus horridus* by reversing many standard features of the *locus amoenus*.

399   **lucus erat** "there was a grove," a classic opening to an atmospheric description of a location in Latin epic poetry, e.g., *lucus in urbe fuit media* Virg. *Aen*. 1.441.

     ab in effect, "since"

400   **aera** Greek acc.

401   **gelidas ... umbras** like *obscurum ... aera*, acc. after *cingens*

     alte summotis solibus abl. absolute, "the sunlight banished far above"

402   **hunc** i.e., *lucus*

     ruricolae noun used adjectivally

     Panes pl. of *Pan*, a rustic god; the pl. suggests a group of deities.

nemorum . . . potentes lit. "powerful over the forests" hence "lords of the forests"

403   **Siluani** pl. of *Siluanus*, i.e., gods associated with the forest

       barbara ritu take the words closely together: "barbarous in ritual"

404   **sacra deum** subject of *tenent*; *deum* = gen. pl. short form, for *deorum*

       structae supply *sunt*

405   **humanis . . . cruoribus** the pl. implies many victims in the rituals of human sacrifice that Lucan locates in this grove; since human sacrifice was obsolete in Rome, this is a mark of brutality and barbarousness here.

       lustrata supply *est*; this carefully crafted line is nearly a "Golden Line"; see 1.3.

406   "if antiquity at all deserves credence for its awe of the gods"; i.e., if we can believe the reports about ancient superstition.

       superos mirata *mirata* agrees with *uetustas*.

407   **illis . . . ramis** emphatic: "upon those branches"

       et either = "even" or looks ahead to the second *et*, "both . . . and"

408   Supply *illis* with *lustris* too.

409   **incubuit** gnomic perf.; sing. because of *uentus*, but *fulgura* is also the subject.

       excussa . . . nubibus atris "shot from black clouds"; cf. 1.151 *expressum uentis per nubila fulmen*, there of Caesar as a force of nature; here Caesar will descend upon the grove like a force of nature.

410-11 Understand as *suus horror inest arboribus* [abl. after *insum*] *praebentibus frondem* [acc.] *non ulli aurae* [dat.]; there are two contrasting ideas here: although the trees expose their foliage to no breeze, the leaves tremble nevertheless.

       non ulli = *nulli*, dat. sing. with *aurae*

suus horror the grove's "shivering" or "trembling" is sinister.

tum not temporal, but marking the "next" element in Lucan's description.

plurima with sing. noun, as often

411-12   **nigris | fontibus** abl. of place whence, i.e., "from"

413   **arte** abl. after *carent*

informia nom. n. pl. agreeing with *simulacra*

caesis extant . . . truncis probably "stand out from the cut-down trunks"; i.e., the images are carved into felled tree trunks.

414   **putri . . . iam robore** "the timber now rotting"

414-15   **facit . . . attonitos** with the acc. pl. Lucan reintroduces people who hold the grove in such awe, continuing with *metuunt* and *timeant*.

415   **non** with *metuunt*

uulgatis sacrata figuris "consecrated with ordinary forms"

416   **tantum** "so much"

addit the subject is *non nosse*, "ignorance of."

417   Understand as *non nosse* [*eos*] *deos quos timeant*; *nosse* = *nouisse*

iam fama ferebat "now it was rumored" + acc. + infin.; Lucan attributes the sinister events in the grove to vague "rumor."

418   **motu terrae** i.e., earthquake

419   **procumbentes . . . consurgere** as the trees start to fall, they mysteriously rise again.

taxos the yew tree, associated with death, was sinister for the Romans; cf. 6.645.

420   Lit. "the fires of a wood that was not burning shone."

421   **robora** object of *amplexos*

circum adv., with *fluxisse*

fluxisse an unusual use of the term, more often applied to liquids

422   **illum** i.e., *lucum*; emphatic by position

       cultu . . . propiore "with worship nearer at hand"

       populi the Gallic tribes around Massilia

423   **cessere** for *cesserunt*, 3rd person pl. pf. act., indicative

       deis dat. after *cessere*

       medio cum Phoebus in axe est "when Phoebus is in mid-sky";
       i.e., even at noon, the priest fears to enter the grove.

424   **sacerdos** a Druid priest

425   **accessus** acc. pl. after *pauet*, in effect, "fears to approach"

       dominum . . . luci by not specifying the identity of "the mas-
       ter of the grove," Lucan makes his description even more sin-
       ister: perhaps no one knows who the terrifying power is; by
       careful ring-composition Lucan closes this section with the
       word it began with, *lucus*.

426-45 Caesar's audacity is partly modeled on Ovid's Erisychthon,
        the god-hating man who in *Metamorphoses* 8 violates the
        grove of Ceres by felling with his axe an ancient oak (*Met.*
        8.738–884). Unlike Erisychthon, Caesar is not punished for
        his sacrilege. This passage ends with a description of the fell-
        ing of the grove in which Lucan mentions five kinds of tree:
        ash, holm-oak, oak, alder, and cypress (440–42). This is Lu-
        can's version of an epic *topos* or set-piece. Usually the trees are
        felled for the funeral pyre of a hero: so Homer, *Iliad* 23.114–
        26; Ennius, *Annales* 175–79 Skutsch; Virgil, *Aeneid* 6.179–82
        and 11.133–38. The Flavian epic poet Silius later reiterates the
        motif (*Punica* 10.524–39), but Ovid and Lucan both bring
        new twists to the *topos*. Ovid substitutes the creation for the
        destruction of a grove at *Metamorphoses* 10.90–105, while Lu-
        can here makes the destruction part of Caesar's personality
        rather than part of a heroic narrative. In all the Latin texts,
        many of the same trees are named, demonstrating the poets'
        awareness of their predecessors.

426   **iubet** i.e., Caesar

inmisso . . . ferro rather than an abl. absolute ("after sending in the steel"), abl. of means, "by sending in the steel"; *ferrum* here must stand for iron axes.

427-28 **uicina, intacta, stabat,** and **densissima** all with **silua** extrapolated from 426; Lucan suggests that Caesar's assault on the sacred grove is driven by vindictiveness.

uicina operi i.e., close to Caesar's siege-works

bello . . . intacta priore perhaps a specific earlier war in the area; for *intacta*, cf. 399 *numquam uiolatus*; even when there had been need of the timber, soldiers had refrained out of religious scruples.

nudatos . . . densissima a powerful contrast; on practical grounds, this "very thick" grove will provide much timber.

429 **fortes . . . manus** i.e., Caesar's soldiers' hands

tremuere for *tremuerunt*, 3rd person pl. pf. act. indicative

moti "affected"; the focus shifts from the soldiers' hands to their emotions.

uerenda gerundive agreeing with *maiestate*, lit. "which ought to be feared," i.e., "awe-inspiring"

430 **si robora sacra ferirent** the conditional clause belongs within the *credebant* clause.

431 **redituras** supply *esse*, making the future infinitive after *credebant*.

432-37 Understand as *ut Caesar uidit, primus ausus* [pf. participle], *effatur* . . . .

432 **inplicitas** the physicality of the word makes the soldiers' fear graphic.

torpore the cause of their "paralysis" is fear.

433 **primus** position emphasizes meaning

raptam . . . bipennem as often with a pf. pass. participle, it works best to make it a finite verb: "he grabbed an axe and balanced it."

librare suggests Caesar's physical control

434   **ausus** Lucan characterizes Caesar as bold.

    aeriam scans as four syllables

    quercum oak trees in epic poetry are often venerable; here Lucan invites us to remember the simile in Book 1 comparing Pompey with an aged oak tree (*quercus*, 1.136): the symbolism is clear.

435   **merso . . . telo** abl. absolute: "after sinking the weapon . . ."

    uiolata in robora here the pf. pass. participle is simultaneous with the action of *merso . . . ferro*; *robora* is pl. for sing.

436   **nequis** introduces a [negative] purpose clause

    uestrum gen. pl. of *uos*, partitive gen.

437   **nefas** Lucan saves the strongest word for the end of Caesar's brief speech; on the flavor of *nefas*, see 1.6.

    omnis separated from its noun, *turba* (439)

438   **imperiis** dat. after *pareo*

    non goes with *secura*

    sublato . . . pauore abl. absolute, "with dread removed"

439   **turba** Lucan's shift from the plural *cohortes* (432) to the singular *turba* indicates that Caesar's troops act as one in response to his orders, an idea underlined by the unanimity of *omnis*.

    expensa superorum et Caesaris ira another abl. absolute, "after weighing the wrath of the gods and the wrath of Caesar"

440   The asyndeton here imitates earlier epic treatments of the tree-felling *topos* (see note on 426–45).

441   **silua . . . Dodones** i.e., oak, referring to the oaks in the oracle of Jupiter at Dodona; *Dodones* is Greek gen. sing.

    fluctibus aptior alnus alder was excellent for making boats; what comparison is implied by *aptior* + dat.? Either more fit for boat-building than other timber or more fit for boat-building than for other purposes, e.g., making weapons.

442   "cypress, witness to no plebeian grief"; i.e., cypress was an expensive wood often used in Roman aristocratic funerals.

luctus acc. pl. for sing.

443   **tum primum** a reminder that the grove is *numquam uiolatus* (399).

posuere for *posuerunt*, 3rd person pl. pf. act. indicative; plural because all the trees named are the subjects.

posuere comas "shed their tresses"; *comas* personifies the trees, intensifying the outrage of the violation.

fronde abl. after *carentes*

444   **admisere** for *admiserunt*, 3rd person pl. pf. act. indicative

444-45 **propulsa . . . cadens** pf. pass. participle agrees with *silua*; the pres. participle *cadens* as usual in Latin denotes action simultaneous with the main verb. The paradox of the felled forest being unable to fall is typical of Lucan; he repeats the idea with corpses unable to fall down because of the crush in battle at 4.787.

robore denso cf. *densissima* 428; either abl. of means with *sustinuit se*, "supported itself with its thick timber" or abl. of location with *propulsa*, "pushed over onto its thick timber."

❧ *The witch Erichtho prepares to perform a necromancy, 6.624–53*

In the middle of the night before the battle of Pharsalia, Pompey's son Sextus consults the Thessalian witch Erichtho about the outcome of the war. In this passage she has just agreed to reveal the future to him through necromancy, that is, prophecy given by a resurrected corpse. Here Lucan describes her selection of a corpse on which to perform the rites of necromancy and the sinister setting for the ritual.

Thessaly was supposed to be home to the most powerful witches. Lucan takes advantage of the location of Pharsalia in Thessaly to include this exciting episode, which is designed to complement and contrast with Aeneas' consultation of the Sibyl in Book 6 of Virgil's *Aeneid*. Where in the *Aeneid* Aeneas goes down to the Underworld, in Lucan's poem the Underworld comes to the upper world.

624   **dixerat** the subject is Erichtho, the witch.

        geminatis arte "doubled by her craft"

625   **tecta caput** f. sing. nom. pf. pass. participle (from *tego*) + acc.
        of respect

626   **corpora caesorum** acc. after *pererrat*; the *caesorum* are "the
        slain," from the pf. pass. participle of *caedo*. Lucan refers to
        corpses here and at 619, although no fighting has yet taken
        place in Thessaly. This may be a sign that the poem is un-
        finished.

        tumulis proiecta negatis Unburied bodies are a repeated mo-
        tif in Lucan, one shared with earlier epic poems, e.g., Hector's
        corpse in Homer's *Iliad* and the bodies of Priam, Misenus, and
        Palinurus in Virgil's *Aeneid*. Here the desecration is increased
        by scavenging wolves and carrion birds (627–28), a reprise of
        Achilles' threats to Hector at *Iliad* 22.345–54.

627   **fugere** for *fugerunt*, 3rd person pl. pf. act. indicative; repeated,
        in initial position, for emphasis

627-28 **reuolsis | unguibus** "after tearing out their talons"

628   **dum** + indicative = "while"

        Thessala adjective used as noun

        uatem her "prophet," the mouthpiece for prophecy

629   **gelidas leto** "chill with death"

        medullas lit. "marrows," for "innards" generally

630   "a stiff lung's lobes, entire, without a wound"; *stantes* (agree-
        ing with *fibras*) indicates that the lung is still intact. It must be
        undamaged so that the corpse can speak.

632   **peremptorum** pf. pass. participle of *perimo*

        multa belongs with *uirorum*, i.e., "the fates of many dead war-
        riors"

        pendent i.e., hang in the balance

633   **quem . . . uelit** indirect question

        superis reuocasse = *reuocauisse*, "to summon back to life
        above"; *superi* usually denotes "the gods."

633-36 A statement of her power: had she wished, she could have raised "entire armies" and the "multitude" inhabiting the Underworld to fight.

634 **temptasset** for *temptauisset*

campis abl. of place where, "on the fields"

acies acc. pl., here in effect "armies"

bello dat. after *reddere*

635 **leges Erebi** Erebus = the Underworld; the "laws of Erebus" prevent the dead from returning to life.

monstro . . . potenti dat. of agent after the pf. pass. participle *extractus*

636 **extractus Stygio . . . Auerno** "drawn from Stygian Avernus." The Styx was one of the rivers in the Underworld hence "Stygian" = "hellish"; Lake Avernus, near Naples, was the entrance to the Underworld used by Aeneas in *Aeneid* 6.

pugnasset for *pugnauisset*

637 **traiecto pectore** Erichtho has thrown a rope around the corpse's chest to drag it along (639).

638 **inserto laqueis feralibus unco** "a hook sunk in the dead man's rope"

640 **uicturum** fut. participle from *uiuere*, denoting purpose, "to live [again]"

montis . . . caui gen. dependent on *rupe* 641

641 **damnarat** = *damnauerat*

sacris probably dat., "to her rites," rather than abl., "by her rites"

642 **caecis** here "hidden"; more often "blind"

depressa describes *humus*, governs the whole line, "sinking almost to the caves of Dis."

643 **in praeceps** "headlong"; *praeceps* is here a noun, more often an adjective.

quam rel. pronoun expanding on *humus*

643-44 **pronis . . . comis** as often in post-Augustan Latin, an abl. phrase is dependent upon an adjective (here, *pallida*).

644-45 **nullo uertice caelum | suspiciens** lit. "looking up at the sky with no top," referring to the yew (*taxus*), which is so dense that it seems to look inward not upward.

645 **Phoebo non peruia** "impenetrable to Phoebus," i.e., to the sun

    taxus like most tree names, this noun is fem.; yew trees were (and still are) associated with death.

647 **longa nocte** explains *pallens*

    nisi carmine factum "unless created by a spell"; *carmen* has a wide range of meanings, ranging from chant or incantation through oracle to song and poem.

648 **habet** has two subjects, *tenebrae* and *situs*, but is attracted into the singular by the second.

    Taenariis . . . faucibus probably abl. of place where: "at the jaws of Taenarus"; Taenarus was a cave in the Peloponnese in Greece which emitted noxious vapors; it was thought to be a gateway to the Underworld.

649 **confine** noun; the entrance to Taenarus constitutes "the boundary" or "limit" between the Underworld and the upper world.

    mundi . . . latentis lit. "the concealed world," "the unseen world," i.e., the Underworld

650 **nostri** supply *mundi* again

    manes acc., object of *admittere*

651 **Tartarei reges** "the kings of Tartarus" are the rulers of the Underworld; Tartarus was the part of the Underworld where punishments were exacted.

    Thessala adjective, with *uates*; contrast 6.628.

652 **uim facit fatis** lit. "applies force to the fates"; on fate in Lucan see 1.33.

652-53 **dubium est . . .** shorthand for *dubium est utrum aspiciat umbras quod traxerit . . . an quod descenderit.* Erichtho is the subject of *aspiciat*; *quod* means "because." The necromancy effaces the sacred boundary between the upper world and the Underworld.

❧ The end of the battle of Pharsalia, 7.617–37

This is one of Lucan's characteristic interventions into his narrative: he is in effect a character in his own poem. Here he laments the scale of the catastrophe, declining to name the individuals who died because the significance of the battle is on a wholly larger scale: it is the death of Rome.

617-30 An enormous sentence, matching the enormity of the catastrophe. Essentially it is a series of indirect questions from 619 onwards, marked by *cuius, quis* (4 times), *qui, quos, quis* (three more times). This is a challenge for the translator, as modern English does not use indirect questions like this; one solution is to render them as direct questions. Lucan evokes the range of deaths that battle can bring, reprising his brilliant treatment of this topic in the sea-battle at Massilia in Book 3 (509–762), culminating here in the particular horrors of civil war, the slaughter of brother and father.

617 **inpendisse** pf. infinitive

pudet governs *inpendisse* and *quaerere*, supply *me*; his "shame" is Lucan's way of apologizing for devoting twenty lines to the death of a single individual, Domitius, ancestor of the emperor Nero, in the preceding lines (not included in this volume).

in funere mundi virtually a temporal clause: "when the world is dying"

618 **mortibus innumeris** dat. after *inpendisse*

singula fata sequentem agrees with unexpressed *me*, lit. "as I follow individual destinies"

619 **per cuius uiscera** the first of the indirect questions: "through whose guts"

620 **fusa solo** lit. "poured on the ground," agrees with *uitalia*, n. pl. adjective used as a noun here

621 **ore . . . aduerso** "facing the enemy"

621-22 Understand as *moriens* [as he died, in the moment of death] *expulerit animā* [drove out with his "breath" or perhaps "life"] *ensem demissum faucibus* [the sword that had been thrust into his throat].

623 **dum** takes pres. indicative when it means "while"

624 **transmittant** Lucan attributes agency to the people suffering the wound: lit. "who send the weapons through their chests"; *pectore* is sing. for pl.

625 **quis** dat. pl., lit. "for which people"

   perruperit aera Lucan evokes the violence of battle with the blood that "splits the air" after the "veins are drained"; *aera* is three syllables.

626 **sui** with *hostis*

   pectora pl. for sing.

627 **notum . . . cadauer** "the familiar corpse."

628 **abscisum . . . mittat** best translated as two verbs: "cuts off and throws away"

629 **nimia . . . ira** "by his excessive wrath"

   spectantibus "to those watching"

630 **quem iugulat** i.e., the victim

   non esse patrem acc. + infinitive after *probet*

630-31 **querella . . . sua** i.e., its own personalized lament

631 **nullos . . . hominum** i.e., "no individuals"

   uacamus the poetic plural, as at 1.2 *canimus*

632-33 Lucan initiates a contrast between the battle of Pharsalia and other battles (lit. "disasters"). Pharsalia, singular subject, governs *habuit*; the verb governed by *aliae clades* (*habuerunt*) is left unexpressed.

633-35 The contrast is made by *illic* (in other disasters) and *hic* (at Pharsalia). First Lucan contrasts *per fata uirorum* and *per populos*: "through the destinies/deaths of [individual] warriors" and "through [entire] peoples." Then, making the same point but in the singular, he contrasts [*mors*] *militis* with *mors . . . gentis.*

635 **ibi** He expands on what happened at other battles.

636 **cunctos . . . cruores** Lucan adds to the types of blood just named that of all nations.

636-37 **haerere, consistere** governed by *uetat.* Lucan's rhetorical point is extreme: the volume of Roman blood prevents all the blood of the other nations "sticking and congealing" on the battlefield.

637 **Romanus . . . torrens** supply *cruoris*: "a torrent of Roman gore"

∾ Pompey concedes defeat and leaves the battlefield, 7.647–82

Pompey finds a vantage-point so that he can survey the disaster unfolding on the battlefield (647–53). He addresses the gods, conceding defeat (654–66), then he departs from the battlefield in a dignified manner (666–82). After this passage, he proceeds to Larisa, a town in Thessaly, where he gets a warm reception. Lucan's account closely follows that of Valerius Maximus (4.55), while Caesar's own account has him hurrying directly to the sea without stopping at Larisa (*Civil War* 3.96).

647 **deos Romanaque fata** subject of *transisse*

648 **uix** take with *coactus*, "reluctantly compelled"

649 Pompey's "fortune" is, like Caesar's "fortune" (1.124), his personal experience of success; as Caesar's fortune rises so Pompey's falls.

650-51 **omnes . . . clades** "all the destruction"

651 **quae ... latebant** of the destruction, which was "hidden from view" until he surveyed it from a vantage-point

652 **sua fata peti** acc. + infinitive after *uidit*: "his own death was the target"

fusa pf. pass. participle from *fundo*, "laid low"

653 **se ... pereuntem** the pres. participle denotes process.

654 **miseris** dat. after *mos est*

trahere supply *eum*, acc. + infinitive after *iuuat*

655 **mersa** agrees with *omnia*, lit. "everything that had been plunged into ruin"

656 **ut ... turbae** the *ut* clause contains the substance of Pompey's prayers, *uotis* (657).

657 **sustinuit . . . credere** "he persisted in believing," followed by acc. (*caelicolas*) + infinitive (*esse*, not expressed).

658 **fouit** "he cherished," my emendation of the manuscripts' *uouit* ("prayed," the idea already expressed in *uotis*, 657) or *uoluit* ("chose" or "desired" from *uelle* or "turned over [in his mind]" from *uoluere*).

sui solacia casus Lucan emphasizes Pompey's magnanimity and sense of responsibility in defeat, in not wishing to destroy "Latium's multitude" by letting them continue to fight for his cause.

659 **parcite** + infinitive, "refrain from"

660 **stante . . . mundo Romaque superstite** two abl. absolutes: "while . . ."

661 **miser** i.e., defeated

si plura iuuant mea uulnera lit. "if more of my wounds please you [gods]," i.e., "if you choose to wound me further"

662 **pignora** here "hostages": it is as if Pompey's wife and sons are the stakes he has placed in his gamble with fate.

663-64 Lit. "is it too little for civil war, if it [civil war] crushes both me and mine?" Pompey suggests that the destruction of himself and his family should satisfy the gods.

664   **exiguae clades sumus** Pompey repeats the idea: "are we [i.e., his family] a trivial disaster?"; the question expects a negative answer.

     orbe remoto abl. absolute, lit. "with the world removed," i.e., without the inclusion of the world as well

665   The shift to 2nd person sing. becomes clear in the next line, with the vocative *Fortuna*.

666   Latin texts are transmitted to us without any punctuation marks; all the punctuation in modern editions is inserted by editors. This line offers a good example of how choice of punctuation can make a difference to meaning and tone. Punctuated as a question ("is nothing now mine?"), Pompey is claiming his life and that of his wife and sons as the only things left to him and offering them to Fortune, in a reproachful tone. Punctuated as a statement ("now nothing is mine"), Pompey is telling Fortune that he has nothing left for her to take from him in a resigned tone of voice.

668   **ruentes** acc. pl.: he "calls back" his troops as they are "rushing" towards their deaths.

669   **se ... negat tanti** "he says he is not worth so much"; *tanti* is gen. of worth.

669–70 Lucan asserts that Pompey's motive was not cowardice. Lit. "Strength was not lacking to the leader to go towards swords and to suffer death in throat or chest."

671–72 Lucan elaborates his earlier point (654–66), that Pompey wished to avoid the destruction of his troops and of "the world."

     strato ... corpore Magni abl. absolute: "once/if Magnus' body lay prostrate"

673   Lucan adds another possible motive for Pompey's withdrawal: to avoid dying in Caesar's sight.

674   **nequiquam, infelix** Lucan again enters his poem, here addressing one of his characters directly. The adjective *infelix* is repeated from 648. Later (9.208) Pompey will be described as *felix*.

     socero ... uolenti dat., after *praestandum est*; supply *tuo*.

675   **ubicumque** stands for a clause, "wherever it may be"

      tu quoque, coniunx Lucan shifts to address Cornelia directly.

675-77   Lucan lists three items that are "the reason for his flight": Cornelia, Cornelia's face, and "the fates' refusal that he should die with part of himself missing." *fatis negatum* is lit. "it having been denied by the fates," followed by unexpressed accusative (*eum*) + infinitive (*mori*); *pur te absente* is another abl. absolute.

678   **sonipes** an elevated word, designed to glorify Pompey's retreat; Caesar's own account has him grabbing a horse and racing away (*Civil War* 3.96).

      pauentem agrees with *Magnum*

      tela the object of *pauentem*

679   **extrema in fata** "towards his final destiny"

      ferentem agrees with *Magnum*

680   **uerendus** supply *est*

681   **qualem** object of *praestare*, referring to *dolor*: "the kind of grief"

↬ *Caesar on the battlefield, 7.728–46*

Now that Pompey has withdrawn to the town of Larisa, Caesar decides to halt the fighting. He addresses his troops, encouraging them to enter and plunder the Pompeians' camp. The soldiers lie down to sleep but are haunted by terrible dreams. Caesar experiences more nightmares than everyone else. Lucan has devised this episode to balance the dream of Pompey with which he started Book 7. His use of dreams and visions is very sparing; as the poem survives, the only other cases are Caesar's vision of Rome in Book 1 and Pompey's dream of Julia at the start of Book 3.

    The next day, Caesar takes breakfast on the battlefield and to prolong the sight of his victory he commands that the dead be left unburied. This is the climax to Lucan's horrific characterization of Caesar as unhuman. Our passage ends with Lucan remonstrating with Caesar for his inhumane behavior.

728   **Hesperio** here "western" means "Italian"

729   **parcendum** impersonal gerundive, supply *esse*, after *ratus*; the verb regularly takes the dative, hence *ferro manibusque*; these are what Caesar has decided to "refrain from using."

730-31 **ut uiles animas perituraque frustra | agmina** The nouns are the objects of *permisit*; *ut* means "as" and gives Caesar's rationale: their souls are "worthless" and the columns of troops would "die to no purpose."

731   **agmina permisit uitae** acc. and dat. after *permitto* can be either way around: here, give the troops to life.

       fugatos i.e., the Pompeians, "who had been routed"

732   **ne** postponed from the start of the clause

734   **Fortuna** for Caesar's special relationship with *Fortuna*, see 1.226.

       dum conficit omnia terror "while terror is all-accomplishing"; cf. the simile of Caesar as a thunderbolt at 1.151–57.

735   **ne** follows *non ueritus*, "not fearing that . . ." or "with no fear that . . ."

       fessis dat., "for the weary" (soldiers)

       Marte subactis "exhausted by war," from *subigo*; like other Latin epic poets, Lucan sometimes uses a god's name metaphorically, e.g., Bacchus = wine, Ceres = grain.

736   **non magno** i.e., moderate, slight

       miles sing. for pl.

737   **ducendus erat** this periphrastic form with the gerundive usually conveys necessity, but here the sense seems to be "was ready/waiting to be led."

737-38 **uictoria nobis | plena** supply *est*: "we have complete victory," "complete victory is ours"

738   **uiri** requires a strong translation such as "warriors."

       superest "there remains," "there is still left"

739   **quam** rel. pronoun, object of *monstrare*

meum est "it is my task," followed by infinitive (*monstrare*)

neque enim donare uocabo Caesar explains why he used the verb *monstrare* rather than *donare*, which would be usual for a general assigning plunder. By doing this, Lucan's Caesar makes his men share in the guilt for the plunder of the Pompeian camp.

740   **plena** takes the abl.

741   **Hesperiis e gentibus** here "western" means Iberian: the Iberian peninsula was a rich source of gold.

742   **Eoas . . . gazas** "treasures from the east" create a polarity with the Spanish gold in the previous line; in Roman thought, the eastern kingdoms (Persia, etc.) were fabulously wealthy.

743   **tot regum fortuna simulque Magni** Caesar refers (a) to the wealthy kings who supported Pompey and (b) to Pompey's personal fortune, which was huge.

       coacta from *cogo*, here "massed"

744   **dominos** "masters," denoting absolute ownership

744-45 **praecedere . . . quos sequeris** supply *eos*: "to get there before the people you are chasing"

745-46 Understand as *opes quascumque Pharsalia fecit tuas rapiuntur a uictis*. Lucan has Caesar appeal to his men's greed; the final position of *opes* makes it emphatic.

       Pharsalia the district in Thessaly where the battle was fought, here the battle itself; see n. on 1.38

∾ *Caesar on the battlefield (continued), 7.760– 811*

760-76 The troops' nightmares replay the battle in a typical case of Lucan doubling back his narrative to heighten its horror.

760   **inpia** a key word in the epic; for Lucan many aspects of civil war are "wicked."

       plebes The idea of "the plebs" sleeping on "patrician turf" is designed to be shocking, an oxymoron, given the long history of conflict between the plebeian and patrician orders in Roman Republican history. Caesar's own account of the civil war mentions the luxurious tents of some of the Pompians, *Civil War* 3.96; cf. Plutarch, *Pompey* 72.

762   **regibus** dat. after *stratum* (from *sterno*), "spread for kings"

miles sing. for pl.

763   **nocentes** Another key word, here used as a noun. They are "guilty" for participating in civil war. Lucan's claim that there were fathers and sons and brothers on opposing sides recalls the opening claim of the poem, that his song is of "wars worse than civil wars," which also refers to Caesar and Pompey being father-in-law and son-in-law.

764   **quos** refers to *nocentes*; translate "them" or "these men."

uaesana quies another oxymoron, since "rest" should be the antithesis of madness.

765   **Thessalicam . . . pugnam** the battle of Pharsalia, which they have just experienced.

miseris dat., lit. "for the wretches," but more comfortably translated as if gen. pl. with *in pectore*, "in the wretches' breasts"; *pectore* is sing. for pl.

766   **inuigilat** another paradox: though the soldiers are asleep, their "savage crime is wide awake."

cunctis another dat., like *miseris* (765)

766-67 **tota | mente** abl. of place where, "in their whole mind," "in all their thoughts," with *mente* sing. for pl.

767   **capulo . . . absente** abl. absolute: "though there is no swordhilt there"

manus nom. pl., subject of *mouentur*

768   **putem** pres. subjunctive, 1st person sing., with a potential aspect: "I could think that . . . ," followed by three acc. + infinitive phrases. The 1st person verb again indicates Lucan's sense of involvement with his narrative.

768-69 **nocentes . . . animas** The "guilty spirits" are the same as the "ghosts" (*manibus*) in the next line, which haunt and torment the sleeping soldiers.

769 **inspirasse** abbreviated form of *inspirauisse*

infectum supply *esse*, pf. infinitive after *putem*

770 **superam . . . noctem** supply *infectam esse*; the "upper night" denotes nighttime in the world above the Underworld.

Stygia a reference to the Styx, the major river of the Underworld; the adjective often refers to the Underworld in general, as in "hellish."

771 **a meritis** pf. participle of the deponent verb *mereor*, lit. "from people who deserve it"; translate "deservedly"

772 **sibila . . . et flammas** the marks of the Furies, with their snaky hair and blazing firebrands

772-73 **perempti | ciuis** "of a murdered citizen": Lucan brings home of horrors of civil war, war against one's fellow-citizens.

773 **sua . . . imago** i.e., his own unique manifestation of mental torment. Lucan continues with a brief catalogue of examples, marked by *ille, ille, hunc, pectore in hoc*, and *in Caesare*.

774 **ille . . . ille** both go with *uidet*

775 **fraterna cadauera** "his brother's corpse," probably pl. for sing., unless Lucan imagines that a brother has killed two siblings.

776 **omnes in Caesare manes** supply *sunt*; Lucan means that all the ghosts (*manes*) that haunt the soldiers individually haunt Caesar collectively.

777-80 Lucan offers comparisons with scenes from tragedy: Orestes being pursued by the Furies after killing his mother; Pentheus' frenzied state of mind when overwhelmed by Bacchus; and his mother Agave's horrified state of mind when she emerged from her Bacchic trance to discover that she had killed her own son.

777-78 The point of comparison is the "faces": *haud alios uidit uultus . . . Orestes*, "no different were the faces that Orestes saw . . ."

777   **nondum Scythica purgatus in ara** eventually Orestes was
        purified at the altar of Diana in the Crimea, here referred to
        as "the Scythian altar"; until then the Furies chased him.

778   **Eumenidum** gen. pl. of *Eumenides*; see 3.15

        Pelopeus Orestes was the great-grandson of Pelops, whose
        name evokes a myth of cannibalism, which perhaps prepares
        us for Caesar's cannibalistic enjoyment of his breakfast on the
        battlefield (786–811).

779   **attonitos** adjective denoting the paralysis of horror, lit.
        "thunderstruck"

        animi subject of *sensere*, referring to the "minds" of Pentheus
        and Agave: lit. "and their minds did not experience thunder-
        struck turmoils any greater [than Caesar did] when Pentheus
        was in the grips of frenzy or when Agave had ceased from her
        frenzy."

        sensere alternative form of 3rd person pl. pf. indicative,
        senserunt

780   **Pentheus** scans as two syllables

        desisset supply *furere*

781   **hunc** Caesar

781–82 **quos aut . . . aut . . .** Caesar is tormented by visions of all the
        swords that the battle of Pharsalia had witnessed (*uidit*) and
        all the swords the day of retribution would bring (*ultrix uisura
        dies*), when he would be murdered in the senate-house.

782   **uisura** supply *est*; periphrastic form of fut. tense

        stringente senatu abl. absolute, using *gladios* as unexpressed
        object, "with the Senate unsheathing [the swords]"

784–86 a tangled thought: "how much of [this] punishment does his
        guilty mind forgive/remit the wretched man [*misero*, dat. af-
        ter *donat*], because he sees the Styx, the shades, and Tartarus
        thrust into his dreams while Pompey is [still] alive (*Pompeio
        uiuente*, abl. absolute)!"; i.e., after Pompey's death, Caesar will
        suffer more acutely.

785 **ingesta** lit. "heaped over," so "thrust upon," with *somnis* (abl.);
acc. pl. agreeing with *Tartara*, but going with the other accusatives *Styga* and *manes* too.

786 **omnia passo** the participle is dat., of Caesar, and *omnia* is the
object of *passo*: lit. "for him having suffered everything."

788 **nulla loci facies** lit. "no appearance of the place," but in effect
the adjective negates the verb *reuocat*, "in no way summons
back."

feralibus aruis dat. after *haerentes*: his eyes are "clinging to
the deathly fields"; Caesar's appetite for the sight of carnage is
part of Lucan's negative characterization.

789 **propulsa** agrees with *flumina*

790 **colles** object of *aequantia*, which qualifies *corpora*

791 **aceruos** i.e., "heaps" of corpses

792 **Magni ... populos** Lucan repeats the idea (from 7.633–35) that
entire nations are involved in Rome's civil war on Pompey's
side.

numerat according to Caesar, 15,000 Pompeians died at the
battle of Pharsalia (*Civil War* 3.99).

epulis Caesar's breakfast on the battlefield, one of the most
macabre moments in the poem, is the climax of Lucan's negative portrayal of Caesar. There is no evidence that this happened; according to Appian, Caesar simply ate Pompey's supper (*Civil Wars* 2.81).

793 **uultus ... faciesque iacentum** beyond representing Caesar's
grisly curiosity, Lucan is making the point that in civil war,
the enemy is someone familiar; *iacentum* is gen. pl.

794 **iuuat** supply *eum*, Caesar: "it delights [him] that he cannot
see ..."

Emathiam ... terram technically Emathia was in Macedonia,
but Lucan uses the adjective to mean Thessaly, the location of
the battle of Pharsalia.

795 **campos sub clade latentes** "fields hidden [lit. hiding, lying
unseen] underneath the carnage"

796   Caesar interprets the slaughter as a sign of supernatural favor. Caesar's faith in his luck has been manifested before; here Lucan caps that with the idea that Caesar sees "his own gods" in his success, as if he has his own personalized deities. This megalomaniacal aspect of Caesar is foregrounded especially in the storm scene in Book 5 (5.504–677).

in sanguine i.e., the blood shed in the battle

797   **furens** a strong word, "in a frenzy" (cf. the comparison with Pentheus at 780), to denote Caesar's outrageous denial of burial to the dead, another unsubstantiated allegation by Lucan, with prototypes in Athenian tragedy.

798   **inuidet igne rogi miseris** the verb *inuideo* can take many different constructions; here we have abl. of the thing refused (*igne*) and dat. of the people denied (*miseris*) (*OLD* 2c).

798-99   **caeloque nocenti | ingerit Emathiam** i.e., "and he forces onto guilty heaven [the sight of] Emathia," with Emathia (on which see above, note on 7.794) standing for the battle of Pharsalia. Lucan calls heaven "guilty" for not preventing this calamity; his Caesar boldly challenges the gods to face the consequences of their inaction.

799-801   Lucan makes a comparison with Hannibal that is to Caesar's disadvantage; the analogy between Caesar and Hannibal is established in Book 1 when Caesar comes over the Alps (1.183) and is compared to a "Libyan lion" (1.226). Understand as *Poenus humator* [i.e., Hannibal] *consulis et Cannae succensae lampade Libycā non illum conpellunt ut seruet ritūs hominum in hoste.* Hannibal is called "the Carthaginian burier of the consul" because after the battle of Cannae in Apulia (South Italy) in 216 BCE, he gave a proper burial to the Roman consul Aemilius Paulus, who was killed in the battle (Livy 22.52.6). The "Libyan torches" are the firebrands used by the Carthaginians, who were from the part of Africa known as Libya.

hominum ritus i.e., "the customs of humanity," lit. "the rites of human beings"

in hoste "in the case of an enemy"

802 **nondum satiata caedibus ira** abl. absolute, "with his anger not yet glutted by the slaughter"; Caesar's rage matches his frenzy (*furens*, 797).

803 **ciues . . . suos** His rage is whetted by the fact that fellow-citizens dared to take up arms against him, so that he hates them even more than he would enemies (*hostes*) from other nations.

803-8 Lucan enters the poem again with apostrophe (i.e., direct address) to Caesar, starting ironically (*petimus . . .*) then offering instructions (*da, urantur, extrue, erige, uideat*).

804 **gentibus** again the idea that entire nations have died fighting for Pompey

805 Lit. "let the bodies be burnt with no flames in between them," i.e., in a holocaust, a single mass burning.

806 **generi si poena iuuat** supply *te*: "if the punishment of your son-in-law delights [you]." Lucan proposes to Caesar that he erect an enormous funeral pyre consisting of the forests from two whole mountains.

  Pindi a mountain on the border of Thessaly.

807 **congestas Oetaeo robore siluas** "the woods packed with Oeta's oak"; Oeta was a mountain in southern Thessaly

808 **ab aequore** i.e., as he flees from Thessaly across the sea

809-10 **tabesne . . . an rogus** indirect question after *haud refert*, "it does not matter," "it makes no difference"

810 **Natura** probably personified, as the Stoic concept of the governing force in the world; the natural decay of bodies matches the view of the atomists (such as Epicureans, including Lucretius), but unlike the atomists the Stoics believed that the souls of the good were purged and then rose into the ether—as happens with the soul of Pompey at the beginning of Book 9.

811 Lit. "bodies owe their own end to themselves," i.e., they decay naturally, they have in them the source of their own demise.

  sui gen. sing. of *se*, after *finem*

∾ *The death of Pompey, 8.542–636*

After he leaves the battlefield, Pompey first sails to Mytilene where he is united with his wife Cornelia and then he consults the Senate, who are accompanying him, about whether to seek refuge in Libya, Egypt, or Parthia. Though Pompey recommends Parthia, the proposal of the senator Lentulus advocating Egypt wins. The first half of Book 8 is designed to show Pompey at his weakest and least commanding. As Pompey's fleet approaches Egypt, the courtiers of the boy-king Ptolemy XIII in Alexandria consider how to receive him. Pothinus the eunuch, a powerful member of Ptolemy's court (see 8.552), advocates Pompey's assassination and the general Achillas is dispatched to carry out the crime.

542-60   This passage starts with Lucan indignantly addressing the gods, then Ptolemy. In his outrage Lucan incorporates many of the various names associated with Egypt (the Nile, Memphis, Pelusium, Canopus, and Pharos) to provoke the characteristic Roman reaction of distrust. He asserts that a civil war ought to be just that, a war between citizens without interference by outsiders. This ironic twist is typical of Lucan; elsewhere he declares a preference for war against foreigners.

542   **Memphis** a town in Egypt

543   **Pelusiaci . . . Canopi** Canopus was a town on the westernmost mouth of the Nile renowned for its luxury; Pelusium was a marshy area on the easternmost mouth of the Nile, but the adjective is often used to mean "Egyptian."

   tam mollis turba an offensive phrase: *turba* implies a mob, out of control, and *mollis* means "effeminate."

544   **hos animos** there is ellipse of a verb such as *habent*.

   fata . . . ciuilia a compressed phrase, meaning "the destiny of civil war"

545   **Romana** n. pl., either an adjective used substantively or agreeing with *fata* (544)

546   **Pharius** adjective derived from Pharos, the island at the mouth of the Nile opposite Alexandria, often used to mean "Egyptian."

547   For a moment Lucan apostrophizes the "civil wars."

548   **monstra** used repeatedly with reference to the court of Ptolemy

549-50   Lucan's thought is that the great reputation of Pompey "the Great" makes it appropriate that he should fall victim to Caesar himself and not to anyone else. Lucan juxtaposes *Magnus* and *Caesar* to underline this.

550   **Caesaris esse nefas** compressed; "to be the crime of Caesar," i.e., to be Caesar's victim

       Ptolemaee Lucan now fiercely addresses Ptolemy (550–60), accusing him of arrogance and ingratitude.

550-51   **tanti ... nominis** again Lucan underlines Pompey's reputation

551   **caelo ... tonante** abl. absolute, "while heaven thunders," indicating the enormous scale of the events unfolding; at such a time, it is inappropriate for Ptolemy to intervene.

552   **inpure ac semiuir** The Romans persistently identified the Egyptian as eunuchs. Although Ptolemy was neither Egyptian (the ruling family were Macedonian in origin) nor a eunuch, he had eunuchs in his entourage, including Pothinus, the courtier who advised Ptolemy to have Pompey killed.

553-56   A complicated thought: even if Pompey's achievements had not been so impressive, all the same he was a Roman and that should have been enough to make Ptolemy desist from attacking him.

553   **domitor mundi** a strong claim that has as its basis Pompey's settlement of the east after his conquest of King Mithridates, in which he made Bithynia, Pontus, and Syria into Roman provinces.

       ter Lucan refers to the three triumphs that Pompey celebrated; see 1.121–23

       Capitolia poetic pl., acc. denoting the destination of the triumphal procession

554   **regum ... potens** the adjective takes the genitive case.

555-56 **Phario satis esse tyranno | quod poterat** The whole phrase
looks ahead to the culminating *Romanus erat*: lit. "the thing
which could have been enough for the Pharian tyrant."

556 **quid** "why?"

uiscera nostra i.e., "Roman guts"

557 **scrutaris** the verb may suggest the physicality of extispicy—
probing the guts of the sacrificed animal.

puer inprobe another derogatory phrase, dismissing Ptolemy
for his youth and his immorality.

558 **iure sine ullo** The reason that Ptolemy holds power "illegally"
is that Pompey had granted him the right to the throne and
that since Pompey has now lost the civil war there is no legal
basis for Ptolemy's position (as Lucan says in 559–60).

560-636 Lucan now narrates the murder of Pompey. The sight of the
small boat that has been sent to meet him fills everyone in
his party with foreboding, but Pompey boards anyway, tell-
ing his wife and son to stay behind, for which Cornelia re-
proaches him. As he steps into the small boat he is greeted by
a Roman mercenary soldier in Ptolemy's pay, at which Lucan
expresses his outrage. Pompey's behavior is depicted as highly
dignified: his self-control is supreme, even after he has been
stabbed. Lucan provides Pompey's dying thoughts in the form
a speech to himself: as earlier in the poem, his thoughts are of
his popularity, fame, and reputation and he consciously be-
haves nobly so as not to damage his popular image.

560 **negarat** plpf., for *negauerat*

562 **quem contra** for *contra quem,* i.e., "to meet whom"; *quem* is
Pompey.

563 **scelerata manus** the subject of *adpellat*; also of *iubet* and
incusat.

Magno dat., after *patere*

564-65 The invitation to transfer from his "lofty vessel's stern into
their small boat" signifies the diminution of Pompey the
Great's status and is an omen of what is to come.

566   **bimarem** the Casian promontory was flanked by bays on ei-
        ther side.

        uadis frangentibus lit. "with the shallows breaking [it]," i.e.,
        the tide, the flow of the sea

567   **qui** rel. clause expanding on *aestum*

568   **quod nisi** "But if . . . not . . . ." Lucan leaves out part of his
        argument: "if the laws of fate . . . were not dragging Magnus
        [he could have escaped because] not one of his companions
        lacked forebodings."

569   **miserae uicinia mortis** *uicinia* is the second subject of *traher-
        ent*; the phrase *intenta . . . iussu ordinis aeterni* expands on
        uicinia: "directed by decree of the eternal order," articulating
        the central Stoic idea of predestination.

570   **damnatum leto** "doomed to death"

571   **ulli** dat. sing., after *derant*

572   **quippe** "the fact is that"

        fides The loyalty inspired by Pompey is one of Lucan's central
        themes in the poem; it includes the loyalty of his wife Corne-
        lia, the loyalty of the people of Larisa and Mytilene who wel-
        come him in defeat, the loyalty of Cordus who later in Book 8
        gives his body a proper burial despite the dangers involved.
        Lucan describes the proper way for Ptolemy to welcome his
        benefactor (574).

573   **sceptrorum auctori** dat., reminding us that Ptolemy owed his
        power to Pompey (see 558–60).

574   **uenturum** supply *fuisse*; the acc. + infinitive represents the
        thoughts of Pompey and/or his entourage.

575   **cedit fatis** the subject is Pompey.

576   Pompey makes a choice between death and fear: in particu-
        lar he does not want to appear to be afraid, which is why he
        chooses to meet his assassins.

577   **praeceps** Cornelia's "headlong" rush to join Pompey is just
        one manifestation of her devotion to him.

578-79 Lit. "not enduring to be absent from her husband as he left, by this much the more, because she feared disaster."

579-82 Pompey forbids his wife and son from joining him in the small boat.

in hac ceruice betrays Pompey's understanding that his life is at risk.

582 **explorate fidem** "test the loyalty": although he knows that he is doomed (see previous note), his words are an encouragement to hope for a better result.

surda uetanti lit. "deaf to him forbidding" her to join him

583 **tendebat** the impf. tense is descriptive or iterative or both.

584-89 Lucan gives Cornelia a reproachful speech, like the one at the end of Book 5 when Pompey has decided to send her away before the battle of Pharsalia (5.762–90), in which she also calls him "cruel" (*crudelis*).

584 **relinquor** pass., "am I left behind"; her complaint recalls that of Ariadne in Catullus 64 when she is abandoned by Theseus.

585 **summota** agrees with implicit *ego*, "I who was kept away from"

numquam omine laeto she means that whenever they are separated, something bad happens to Pompey.

586 **miseri** the m. pl. includes both Pompey and Cornelia; this generalization to the masculine is standard in Latin.

587 **cum fugeres alto** "when you were fleeing across the deep," a poetic way of referring to the sea

relinquere like *flectere*, after *poteras*, "you could have left me"

Lesbi She refers to the fact that Pompey sent her away to Mytilene, the main city on the island of Lesbos, to keep her safe during the campaign in Greece.

588 She is reproaching him for collecting her from her "hiding-place on Lesbos" if it was his intention to prevent her from making any other landfall with him, e.g., in Egypt.

589 **an tantum in fluctus placeo comes** lit. "or do I please you as a companion only for the waves?"

590 **prima . . . puppe** "the vessel's end"; the *puppis* was the stern, though the word is often used by metonymy to denote the entire ship.

593 **ad ducis euentum** "about their general's fate"

 metuens By specifying the form of their fear, Lucan produces another surprise: they are afraid not of the violent crime (expressed with simple accusatives) but of Pompey disgracing his reputation (expressed with a *ne* clause).

595 **sceptra sua donata manu** repeats the point of 558–60 and 573

 transire parantem a true pres. participle: "as he was preparing to step across," into the small Egyptian boat

596 **Romanus** Initial position in the line carries emphasis: it is shocking that a Roman soldier would undertake the assassination of a Roman general. According to other sources, Septimius had served as a centurion under Pompey in the campaign to clear the Mediterranean of pirates (Caesar, *Civil War* 3.104; Plutarch, *Pompey* 78).

597 **Septimius** postponed for dramatic impact

 pro superum pudor *pro* is an interjection marking shock or surprise, followed by a variety of constructions, including the nom. as here.

598 **regia . . . deformia** both acc. pl. agreeing with *arma*

 posito . . . pilo abl. absolute, "the javelin having been put aside"; as often, it works better to switch from passive to active and to make this a second finite verb, "he had put aside the javelin and . . . ." The *pilum* was the characteristic weapon of the Roman legionary: see 1.7.

599-600 Lucan heaps up epithets in condemnation of Septimius.

 nulla . . . ferarum abl. of comparison, f. because of *fera*; lit. "than none of the wild beasts"

in caedes "for bloodshed," "for slaughter"

600   **quis non . . . putasset** for *putauisset*; the plpf. is rare with the potential subjunctive; *non* is the regular negative in potential clauses.

Fortuna Lucan addresses Fortune for the next few lines, and then Pompey himself, thus slowing down and delaying his narrative of the murder, to which we return at 610.

601   **parcere . . . populis** lit. "spare the peoples," i.e., take pity on the world, by keeping the mercenary soldier Septimius out of the civil war.

bello haec dextra uacaret "this hand had no part in war," i.e., Septimius' sword-hand; *bello* is abl. after *uacaret*.

602   **Thessalia** abl. of separation, with *procul*

fugasses for *fugauisses*, transitive verb with *tela* as object

603–4   Lucan asserts that Fortune has stationed Roman swords everywhere, including in Egypt, so that acts of civil warfare—i.e., against fellow-citizens—can be performed everywhere.

604   **heu** an interjection denoting emotion, regret

605   **dedecus** supply *est*, "it is a disgrace"; the substance of the "disgrace" and "the story" comes in the two clauses that follow, *Romanus . . .* and *Pellaeus . . . .*

caritura nom. sing. fut. participle of *careo*, agreeing with *fabula*

pudore abl. after *caritura*

606   **regi** dat. after *paruit*, from *pareo*

607   **Pellaeus . . . puer** The boy-king Ptolemy; Pella, the birthplace of Alexander the Great, was in Macedon, so *Pellaeus* often means "Macedonian": the Ptolemies were descended from Alexander's general Ptolemy.

tibi dat. of disadvantage, almost the same as saying *tua colla*

608   **tuo** The sword used to cut off Pompey's head is "his own" in the sense that Septimius had served under Pompey: see 596.

608–9   **qua . . . fama** "with what reputation"

609   **quo nomine dicent** lit. "with what name shall they speak," i.e., "how shall they name," "what will they call"

610   **qui Bruti dixere nefas** compressed: "who have called [the act] of Brutus a crime," a reference to the assassination of Julius Caesar by Brutus and his accomplices. In Lucan's value system, the murder of Pompey is ineffably worse than the murder of Caesar.

       dixere for *dixerunt*, 3rd person pl. pf. act. indicative

610-12 Pompey's loss of agency, which Lucan here describes, is matched by the grammatical passivity of *ablatus in alnum*, "carried off into the boat."

612   **iura sui** lit. "laws over himself," *sui* being gen. sing. of the pronoun *se*

613   **regia monstra** "the monsters of the king," referring to the assassins; *monstra* makes them subhuman.

614   **uultus** pl. for sing.

       apertum agrees with *caput* in the next line.

615   **praebere** infinitive after *indignatus*

       caput the second object of *inuoluit*

       pressit from *premo*, here "to close"

616-17 **nequas effundere uoces | uellet** lit. "lest he should have the wish to pour out any utterances"

617   **aeternam . . . famam** Pompey's awareness of his reputation is one of his main driving forces, according to Lucan.

618   **Achillas** the general of Ptolemy who was given the job of assassinating Pompey

619   **nullo gemitu** The phrase is given prominence by initial position as Lucan emphasizes Pompey's self-control at the moment of death. It belongs with both *consensit* and *respexit*.

621   **seque probat moriens** "and as he dies he tests himself"

       haec in pectore uoluit Lucan here imagines Pompey's dying thoughts (622–35), making this an opportunity to reinforce his characterization.

622　**numquam tacitura labores** "that will never be silent about the toils"; *tacitura* is fut. participle of *taceo*, agreeing with *saecula*.

623　**sequens** "future," lit. "following"

624　**ratem Phariamque fidem** The adjective goes with both nouns. Pompey characteristically measures what is happening in terms of "loyalty."

　　consule famae imperative: Pompey is addressing himself; *consulo* takes the dat. of the thing thought about; typically, he is concerned about his posthumous reputation.

625　**prospera** in apposition, almost as an adverb after the verb, "have flowed successful[ly]"

626　**populi** Pompey is confident that "the peoples" of the world will judge his behavior and this makes him determined to "prove himself in death."

　　probaris 2nd person sing., pres. pass.

627　**scieris** pf. subjunctive of *scio* after *an*, marking an indirect question; *scio* + infinitive meaning "know how to" is common.

　　aduersa n. pl. acc., the object of *pati*, pres. infinitive from *patior*

　　ne cede . . . dole a prose author would write *noli cedere . . . dolere*.

　　pudori the shame derives from being killed at the instigation of the Egyptians.

628　**quacumque** supply *manu* from *manum* in the next line: "by whatever hand"

629　**crede manum soceri** supply *esse*; Pompey can cope better with the situation if he imagines that Ptolemy is acting on the orders of Caesar, his "father-in-law."

　　spargant lacerentque supply *me* as object

　　licebit a common Latin idiom, "although," with the subjunctive; more often *licet*, pres. tense

630–31　**nulli . . . potestas | hoc auferre deo** supply *est*, lit. "there is to no deity the power to take this away," i.e., "no deity has the power to take this away" [from me]

631-32   To rise above the changes of fortune in life was a central aim of the Stoic philosophy, to which Lucan subscribed.

631   **prospera** n. pl. as noun, subject of *mutantur*

         uita abl., "in life"

633   **Pompeius ... meus** his son Sextus

         tanto "by so much the more," with the comparative adverb *patientius*

634   **claude ... gemitus** "suppress your groans"

         dolor to encourage himself, Pompey addresses his "pain."

         peremptum supply *me*, "me dead," "me in death." The word is the object of both *mirantur* and *amant*: Pompey equates admiration with devotion. He cannot imagine them loving him if he behaves dishonorably and gives way to the pain.

635   **Magno** dat. of possession, with *erat*: "Magnus had ..."

636   **mentis** after *custodia*

         animi morientis gen. after *ius*, "power over"

∾ *The death of Pompey (continued), 8.663–88*

The narrative of Pompey's murder resumes after Cornelia has delivered another impassioned speech, which echoes a speech earlier in Book 8 (lines 88–105), blaming herself for Pompey's fate and showing her devotion to him by wishing to join him or even precede him in death. The Roman mercenary severs Pompey's head and gives it to Achillas so it can be presented to Ptolemy, who goes on to have it embalmed, a custom the Romans regarded as barbaric. The passage ends with another case of Lucan expressing his outrage.

664   **permansisse** pf. infinitive after *fatentur* (666)

665   **placatam** I prefer this emendation (taken from Shackleton Bailey's 1988 Teubner text) to the manuscripts' *iratam* because it enhances Pompey's majesty to be reconciled to his fate rather than "raging at the gods."

nil short form of *nihil,* object of *mutasse*

ultima mortis lit. "the last things of death," translate "utmost death" or "the finality of death"

666 **mutasse** another pf. infinitive, short form of *mutauisse*

667 **qui** supply *ei* with *fatentur*

uidere for *uiderunt,* 3rd person pl. pf. act. indicative

668 **Septimius sceleris maius scelus** Lucan's juxtaposition of *scelus* in two different cases with the Roman soldier's name conveys his disgust. *sceleris* is gen. after *actu.* The "discovery of a greater crime" fits Lucan's tendency to take the horror to the next point on the scale wherever possible.

669 **sacros . . . uultus** Lucan virtually deifies Pompey; cf. Book 9, which opens with Pompey's apotheosis; *uultus* is pl. for sing.

scisso uelamine as Lucan told us at 614–15, Pompey "covered his face and head" before he was struck; Septimius here "tears away the covering."

670 **semianimis**, **spirantia** with these details Lucan ratchets up the horror: Pompey is not yet fully dead when he is decapitated; *semianimis* scans as four syllables, the first *i* being consonantal.

ora another pl. for sing.

671 **colla** again, pl. for sing.

in obliquo . . . transtro as often with Latin adjectives of position (e.g., *medius, summus*), the phrase needs unpacking in English: "across a bench."

673 **diu** lit. "for a long time"; Lucan means that it takes him a long time to sever the head.

nondum artis erat caput ense rotare Lucan is sarcastic, implying that in his own day it had already become "an art to send a head rolling with the sword," i.e., to decapitate at a single stroke. *artis* is a partitive gen., i.e., "an element of skill."

674 **abscisa recessit** the two words reinforce, almost reiterate, one another, an intensifying device favored by Lucan.

675   **Pharius . . . satelles** i.e., Achillas

      dextra gestare explains *hoc*

676-78   Lucan enters his poem to reproach Septimius for not following
         through to its logical conclusion his decapitation of Pompey.

676   **operae . . . secundae** gen. of description, "in a supporting role"

677   **sacrum caput** as at 669

678   **o summi fata pudoris!** The gen. phrase explains what Pompey's
      "destiny" consists of: Lucan here anticipates the next outrage,
      that Pompey's head is stuck on a spear and taken to Ptolemy.

679   **nosset** short form of *nouisset*, plpf. subjunctive, which is
      translated as if impf. tense.

679-80   **uerenda | regibus** "which should be revered by kings"; their
         king, however, is showing no such respect.

680   **generosa fronte** probably abl. of place where, "on his noble
      brow"

      decora nom. sing. agreeing with *caesaries* (681); the noun may
      evoke Caesar's name here, as at 1.189.

682   **uultus** pl. for sing. again

      in murmura lit. "into murmurs"; translate "to murmur"

683   **singultus animae** pl., subject of *pulsant*, "sobs of breath"

      nuda in another sign of disrespect, no one has closed Pompey's
      eyes.

684   **suffixum caput est** goes with *ueruto* (681)

      quo . . . bella iubente rel. clause expanding on *caput*

      numquam goes with *pax fuit*: Lucan asserts Pompey's power
      to determine whether the Roman state would be at war or at
      peace.

685   **hoc** i.e., *caput*; another reference to Pompey's power in Ro-
      man life

      Campum i.e., the Campus Martius ("Field of Mars"), the area
      of Rome where elections were held

      rostra the platform from which speeches were delivered by
      politicians

686 **Fortuna . . . Romana** Lucan briefly apostrophizes "Roman Fortune," asserting that she "was pleasing to herself" through Pompey, i.e., that Rome could be proud of her achievements thanks to Pompey.

❧ Cato's funeral oration for Pompey, 9.190–217

Lucan opens Book 9 with the apotheosis of Pompey: his spirit leaves his ashes and flies up to the abodes of the blessed. This episode shows once again Lucan's devotion to his far from perfect hero. Then Cato, Pompey's senatorial ally and the moral touchstone of the poem, delivers a funeral oration in praise of Pompey. Cato the Younger, who was introduced in Book 2 as an austere Stoic, became the leader of the Republican cause after Pompey's death. Much of Book 9 focuses on his powers of endurance, establishing him as the replacement for Pompey in the narrative; we can assume that Lucan planned a major role for him in the remainder of the poem, which might perhaps have culminated with his Stoic-style suicide at Utica after the battle of Thapsus (46 BCE), in preference to falling into Caesar's hands alive. Cato's suicide is an episode celebrated by Lucan's uncle, the Stoic philosopher Seneca, e.g., *Moral Letters* 24.6–8; *On Providence* 2.9–12; *On Firmness* 2.

    Cato's funeral oration, delivered at his camp in Africa once Cornelia and Pompey's sons have joined him, is relatively brief, resembling a Roman epitaph (grave inscription). It is no obsequious eulogy; rather, its praise is balanced with criticisms, which make it seem more sincere. Though grudging, Cato's admiration shows through.

190 **ciuis** Cato starts his tribute by firmly labeling Pompey "a Roman citizen," implying his loyalty to the Roman state.

    obit from *obeo*, gives us the word "obituary"

    multum adv. with *inpar*

191 **nosse** short form of *nouisse*, pf. infinitive, with pres. force; the infinitive follows *inpar*, "inferior at knowing"

192 **cui** refers to *aeuum*

fuit the pf. tense is used for generalizations

iusti gen. n. sing. of *iustum*, "justice," after *reuerentia*, "respect for"

192-93 **salua | libertate** abl. absolute in the pres. tense: Cato is saying that Pompey was "powerful" (*potens*) "without harming liberty," lit. "with liberty [still] safe"; the implicit contrast is with Caesar, whose power destroyed the liberty of the Roman state, according to Lucan.

193-94 The syntax is compressed: "when the plebs was ready (abl. absolute) to be slaves to him, [Pompey] was (*erat*, 195) the only one [to be] a private citizen," i.e., to seek no public position to underpin his power. Again, the contrast is with Caesar, who continually sought public office. *priuatus* is almost a technical term, denoting someone who holds no public office.

194-95 **rector . . . senatus, | sed regnantis, erat** again, compressed: Cato describes Pompey as "the ruler of the Senate" (which no individual was supposed to be) but qualifies this criticism with the concession that at that time the Senate was still exercising power, lit. "ruling," gen. sing. of the pres. participle of *regno*; this produces the play on words *rector . . . regnantis.*

195 **poposcit** from *posco*

196 Supply *ea* as subject of *negari*: "what he wanted to be given [to him], [those things] he wanted to be able to be denied to him"; use *sibi* in both clauses. *dari* and *negari* are both pres. pass. infinitives. Cato is saying that Pompey at least subscribed to the theory that the Roman state was free to refuse any requests he might make.

197 **inmodicas possedit opes** another criticism, especially coming from the Stoic Cato; Stoicism commended a simple or even ascetic lifestyle with no concern for material goods.

plura retentis lit. "more things than the things kept back"

198 **intulit** "paid in," i.e., to the state treasury

inuasit ferrum sed ponere norat another criticism which is immediately balanced: "he did seize the sword, but knew how to put it down." *ponere* is simple verb for compound (e.g., *deponere*); *norat* is the short form of *nouerat*, plpf. with impf. sense.

199 **togae** i.e., "peace"; the characteristic garb of the Roman citizen (as opposed to the Roman soldier) metaphorically denotes "peacetime," as at 1.130.

armatus "once armed"

200 **potestas** the subject of both instances of *iuuit*, which is the irregular (and unusual) pf. tense of *iuuo*

201-2 supply *ei erat*, lit. "there was to him," i.e., "he had . . ."; *domus* (f. sing.) is qualified by *casta* and *carens* (+ abl. *luxu*) and *corrupta*.

202 **fortuna** meaning "prosperity," "success"

202-3 Three expressions describe Pompey's *nomen* (supply *est* or *erat*), *clarum*, then *uenerabile . . . gentibus*, then the relative clause (with *quod* postponed). Pompey's great name is a major obsession of Lucan. By *gentibus* Lucan is thinking especially of the eastern nations and Pompey's eastern settlement.

203 **multum** adv. with *proderat*

quod i.e., *nomen*

204-6 Another negative formulation: Lucan has Cato say that in the era of Marius and Sulla, who competed for power at Rome some forty years earlier, "the true guarantee of liberty disappeared," but that with Pompey's death "even the bogus guarantee has gone." The fierce competition for power between Marius (with his repeated consulships) and Sulla (who made himself dictator) was the beginning of the process that led to the civil war between Caesar and Pompey, partly through the phenomenon of powerful men raising armies that had greater loyalty to their commanders than to the state. Lucan incorporates an old man's lengthy reminiscences of the civil wars between Marius and Sulla at the beginning of Book 2 (2.16–33). Our sources sometimes map Caesar onto Marius (because he was a relative of his) and Pompey onto Sulla (because he served under Sulla).

204 **Sulla Marioque receptis** abl. absolute, with the participle in the abl. pl.: "once Sulla and Marius had been admitted [to power]"

205 **Pompeio rebus adempto** another abl. absolute, with *rebus* (dat. of disadvantage) meaning "from the world"; *adempto* is pf. pass. participle from *adimo*.

206 **non iam regnare pudebit** impers., lit. "now it will be no cause for shame to rule"; *regnare* here has a strong sense connected with *rex*, which for the Romans denoted an autocrat or tyrant.

207 **erit** goes with both *nec* phrases: "there will not be . . ."

frons . . . senatus *senatus* is gen. sing., "outward show consisting of the Senate"

208 **felix** the reason for Pompey's good fortune, according to Lucan, is that he did not continue to live under Caesar's tyranny.

obuia translate "to meet him"

uicto lit. "to him having been defeated," dat. after *obuia*

209 **quaerendos** the gerundive has a strong sense of obligation: "which he should have sought out" on his own initiative.

enses poetic plural

210 **potuisses** Lucan's Cato addresses the dead Pompey directly, borrowing Lucan's own habit of apostrophe.

regno "tyranny"; on the negative flavor of *regnum* and *regno*, see 9.206.

211 This line forms a *sententia*, i.e., a pithy and memorable generalization, part of the rhetorical apparatus of imperial Roman writers.

scire mori the complement of *sors*

sors prima supply *est*; *prima* almost = *optima* here

uiris dat. pl., "for warriors"

proxima also with *sors*

cogi pres. pass. infinitive, after *scire*; supply *mori* after *cogi*

212 Cato hypothetically puts himself in the same position, of falling "into another's power," meaning Caesar's; he addresses

the goddess Fortuna with the request that Juba, the king of Numidia and another ally of Pompey, might do the same as Ptolemy and kill him [Cato] first.

213 **hosti** dat. after *seruari*

dum + subjunctive, "provided that"

214 **seruet** the implicit subject is Juba

ceruice recisa i.e., "with my head cut off"

215-17 Lucan claims that Cato's diluted praise for Pompey counted for more than the standard funeral eulogies delivered in the Roman forum at the rostrum, implying that to win the stern Cato's approval was difficult.

215 **maior** with *honor*, 217

217 **mortis honos** "honor in death"

❧ *Caesar at the site of Troy, 9.961–99*

Lucan scrolls back in time to immediately after the battle of Pharsalia. Caesar sets out in pursuit of Pompey but stops at Troy, where he goes sightseeing with a local guide (the *Phryx incola* and *monstrator* mentioned below, 976–79), visiting places mentioned in the story of the Trojan War, especially in Homer's *Iliad*. The site is in decay, but Caesar prays to the gods of Troy, promising them the restoration of their citadel if they make him successful. This invented episode, as well as appealing to the antiquarianism of Lucan's audience, is designed to emphasize Julius Caesar's descent from the Trojan founder of the Roman race, Aeneas, through his son Iulus, whose name evokes both Ilium (one of the Greek names for Troy) and Caesar's clan name Iulius. This passage includes Lucan's apostrophe to Caesar, promising him immortality through Lucan's poem, a bold claim by the young epic poet.

961 Sigeum was a promontory near Troy.

962 **Simoentis** gen. sing. of *Simois*; a river running near Troy

busto abl. after *nobile*

963   Rhoeteum was a place near Troy famous for the tomb of the
       Greek warrior Ajax.

       The "ghosts owe much to the bards" because poets such as
       Homer immortalized the warriors who fought at Troy in po-
       ems such as *Iliad*.

964   **nomen memorabile** again Lucan's concern with fame is
       exhibited.

965   **magna** the epithet is transferred from *muri* to *uestigia*

       Phoebei . . . muri Apollo with Neptune built the city-wall of
       Troy for King Laomedon.

966   **putres robore** lit. "rotten in their wood"

967   **Assaraci** king of Phrygia, son of Tros, grandfather of Anchis-
       es, great-grandfather of Aeneas

       pressere for *presserunt*, 3rd person pl. pf. act. indicative

968   **iam lassa radice** "with roots now weary" because this has
       been the situation for so long.

969   **Pergama** the citadel of Troy

       etiam periere ruinae "ruins" should not be able to be de-
       stroyed further; this is a surprise typical of Lucan; *periere* is
       for *perierunt*, 3rd person pl. pf. act. indicative.

970   **Hesiones** Greek gen. sing.; the "rock" was where Hesione,
       daughter of Laomedon, king of Troy, was exposed to a sea-
       monster and rescued by Hercules.

       silua "in the wood[s]"

971   **Anchisae thalamos** the place on Mount Ida where Anchises
       and Venus made love; their son was Aeneas.

971-73 Three relative clauses after *aspicit* (970), introduced by *quo*,
       unde, and *quo*.

971   **quo . . . antro** i.e., *aspicit antrum quo*, "the cave in which . . ."

       iudex "the adjudicator" is the Trojan Paris, passing judgment
       on the beauty of the three goddesses Juno, Minerva, and Ve-
       nus (hence "the judgment of Paris"), again on Mount Ida.

972   **puer** Ganymedes, son of Tros, abducted by Jupiter to be his cupbearer and lover

raptus supply *sit*, pf. pass. subjunctive

caelo "to heaven"

quo uertice i.e., *aspicit uerticem quo*, "he sees the peak on which . . ."; the peak is Mount Ida, some way from the city.

973   **luxerit** pf. subjunctive of *lugeo*

Oenone a nymph (Naiad) loved by Paris; after he deserted her for Helen, she refused to heal his battle-wound and he died, which made her grief-stricken.

nomine lit. "name" (again), almost "story"

975   **Xanthus** a river near Troy

976   **manes** pl. for sing.

978   **seruantia** pres. participle agreeing with *saxa*

979   **Herceas . . . aras** poetic pl.; the inner altar in Priam's palace where Neoptolemus/Pyrrhus killed him (as narrated in *Aeneid* 2); when Zeus (= Jupiter) was viewed as the god of the house in Greek cult he was called Zeus Herkeios.

980   **uatum** Lucan's exclamation about the importance of "the work of bards" is a preliminary to his intimations of his own literary immortality.

fato abl. of separation after *eripis*; "death," i.e., "oblivion"

981   **aeuum** lit. "age" or "time," hence "immortality"

982-86 Lucan addresses his anti-hero, Caesar, in a tone of intimacy, promising him literary immortality to match that of the Homeric heroes.

982   **inuidia** abl.

sacrae . . . famae those immortalized by poets such as Homer enjoy "sacred fame."

tangere 2nd person sing. pass. pres. imperative, with *ne*; a prose author would write *noli tangi*.

983   **siquid** object of *promittere*

Latiis . . . Musis dat. after *fas est*; Lucan means "Latin poets."

984   **Zmyrnaei . . . uatis** Homer, who was said (according to some) to have been born at Smyrna on the west coast of Asia Minor.

honores i.e., the honors bestowed on Homer, but also the honors bestowed by him.

985   Lucan omits the correlative to *quantum*, i.e., "so much," "so long."

uenturi m. pl. nom. fut. participle used as a noun: "people in the future," "future ages"

Pharsalia nostra i.e., the battle of Pharsalia as won by Caesar and recorded by Lucan; some have taken this line to mean that Lucan called his poem *Pharsalia*.

986   **tenebris** dat. after *damnabimur*

988   **subitas** English would use an adverb not an adjective here.

989   **non inrita** litotes; the phrase goes with *uota*, looking to the future.

990-99 Fully half of Caesar's prayer consists of invocations to the deities that make the strongest connection between Troy and Rome—and also between Troy and Julius Caesar, given his purported descent from the Trojan Aeneas.

990   **di cinerum** short form of *dei* with gen. pl. of *cinis*

quicumque m. pl. nom., with *di*, i.e., whichever are the gods "that inhabit the ruins of Troy"

991   **Aeneae . . . mei** gen. sing., after *lares* (992); Julius Caesar claimed descent from Aeneas through Iulus, Aeneas' son (hence, supposedly, the family name Iulius).

quos rel. clause expanding on the postponed noun *lares*

Lauinia sedes i.e., the city of Lavinium in Latium, which was founded by Aeneas.

992   **Alba** i.e., Alba Longa, another ancient town in Latium, founded by Aeneas' son Iulus/Ascanius and home of the house-gods brought from Troy by Aeneas.

quorum the rel. clause expands upon *lares*

993 **ignis . . . Phrygius** the flame brought by Aeneas to Italy, never extinguished (*lucet . . . adhuc*)

nulli . . . uirorum dat. of agent after the pass. participle *aspecta*, with partitive gen., "by no male"

994 **Pallas** the image of the goddess Pallas Athena, known as the Palladium, which was the emblem of the safety and continuity of Troy, kept in the temple of Vesta at Rome.

995 **gentis Iuleae** Caesar specifies his clan name because that is what links him to Troy (see 991).

997 **date** the imperative is almost a conditional, "if you grant me . . . I shall restore . . ."

in cetera lit. "into the rest," i.e., "for the future"

998 **grata uice** "in grateful reciprocation"; i.e., just as Rome's walls were built by Trojans, so Troy's walls will be rebuilt by Romans.

999 The line consists almost entirely of names, with powerful juxtapositions designed to underline Rome's foundation from Troy.

Ausonidae an elevated way of referring to the people of Ausonia, i.e., Italians

Romana . . . Pergama Lucan perhaps hints at Caesar's alleged plan to make Troy or Alexandria the capital of the empire (Suetonius, *The Deified Julius* 79.3).

Vocabulary

ā *or* **ab,** *prep.* + *abl.,* from, away from; by (*agent*)

abeō, -īre, -iī or **-iuī, -itum,** to go away

abscīdō, -ere, abscindī, abscīsum, to cut off

absens, -entis, *adj.,* absent, missing

abstrūsus, -a, -um, *adj.,* hidden

abstulī. *See* **auferō**

ac. *See* **atque**

accēdō, -cēdere, -cessī, -cessum, to approach; attack; be added to

accendō, -ere, -cendī, -cēnsum, to burn, kindle

accessus, -ūs, *m.,* the act of approaching, approach, visit

ācer, ācris, ācre, *adj.,* fierce, keen

aceruus, -ī, *m.,* heap, pile

Achaeus, -a, -um, *adj.,* Achaean

Acherōn, -tis, *m.,* Acheron, a river in the Underworld

Achillās, -ae, *m.,* Achillas

aciēs, -ēī, *f.,* battle line; gaze, vision

actum, -ī, *n.,* deed, action

actus, -ūs, *m.,* act

ad, *prep.* + *acc.,* to, towards

addō, -ere, addidī, additum, to add (to), intensify + *dat.*

adfīgō, -fīgere, -fīxī, -fīctum, to fix, fasten to

adflīgō, -ere, -flīgī, -flīctum, to damage, injure, afflict

adimō, -ere, -ēmī, -ēmptum, to take away

admittō, -ere, -mīsī, -missum, to admit, allow

adōrō (1), to supplicate, adore, kneel before

adpellō. *See* **appellō**

adstō, -āre, -stitī, —, to stand by, stand near

adsum, -esse, -fuī, —, to be present, be here

adūrō, -ere, -ussī, -ūstus, to burn, scorch

aduersus, -a, -um, *adj.,* opposite, facing; adverse

Aegaeus, -a, -um, *adj.,* Aegean

Aegyptus, -ī, *f.,* Egypt

aemulus, -a, -um, *adj.,* rivaling, vying with

Aenēās, -ae, *m.,* Aeneas

aequō (1), to equal, be as high as

aequor, -oris, *n.,* plain; sea

āēr, āeris, *m.,* air, sky

āerius, -a, -um, *adj.,* in the air, tall

aestās, -tātis, *f.,* summer

aestifer, -era, -erum, *adj.,* heat-bringing, torrid

aestuō (1), to boil, blaze

aestus, -ūs, *m.,* surge, swell, tide

aeternus, -a, -um, *adj.,* eternal, everlasting

aethēr, -eris, *m.,* sky, upper air, ether

Aetna, -ae, *f.,* Etna, a volcano in Sicily

aeuum, -ī, *n.,* age, era, time

Agāuē, -ēs, *f.,* Agave, mother of Pentheus

ager, agrī, *m.,* field, countryside

agger, -eris, *m.,* mound

agito (1), to drive, harass

agmen, -inis, *n.,* crowd, horde

agnoscō, -ere, -nōuī, -nitum, to recognize

agō, agere, ēgī, actum, to act, do, achieve; drive

āiō, *defective verb,* to say

Alba, -ae, *f.,* the city of Alba Longa

aliēnus, -a, -um, *adj.,* belonging to another

alius, -a, -ud, *adj.,* other

alnus, -ī, *f.,* alder; boat [made of alder-wood]

Alpēs, -ium, *f.pl.,* the Alps

altāria, -ium, *n.pl.,* burnt-offerings

altē, *adv.,* at/to/from a great height, far above; at/to a great depth

alter, -era, -erum, *pron.,* one (of two), the other

altum, -ī, *n.* the sea, deep water

altus, -a, -um, *adj.,* high; deep

āmens, -entis, *adj.,* frantic, distracted

amnis, -is, *m.,* river

amō (1), to love

amor, -ōris, *m.,* love

amplector, -ctī, amplexus, to clasp, embrace, encircle

amplexus, -ūs, *m.,* embrace

an, *conj.,* + *subj.,* whether, or

Anchīsēs, -ae, *m.,* Anchises, father of Aeneas

angustus, -a, -um, *adj.,* narrow, short

anima, -ae, *f.,* breath, life; soul

animus, -ī, mind, spirit, courage; anger, arrogance

annus, -ī, *m.,* year

antīquus, -a, -um, *adj.,* old, ancient

antrum, -ī, *n.,* cave, cavern

anxius, -a, -um, *adj.,* anxious

aperiō, -īre, -uī, -ertum, to open, reveal, uncover

appellō (1), to address, speak to

appellō, -ere, -ulī, -ulsum, to put in (of ships)

apsēns. *See* **absēns**

aptus, -a, -um, *adj.,* fit, ready, suitable, convenient

aquila, -ae, *f.,* eagle; standard

āra, -ae, *f.,* altar

Araxēs, -is, *m.,* a river in Armenia

arbor, arboris, *f.,* tree

arceō, -ēre, -uī, —, to ward off, keep away

ardens, -entis, *adj.,* burning, fiery, hot

arma, -orum, *n.pl.,* weapons,
arms

armātus, -a, -um, *adj.,* armed,
in armor

ars, artis, *f.,* art, skill, craft

Arsacidae, -ārum, *m.pl.,*
descendants of Arsaces

aruum, -ī, *n.,* field

asper, -era, -erum, *adj.,* harsh,
rough, rugged

aspiciō, -ere, -spexī, -spectum,
to look at, see

Assaracus, -ī, *m.,* Assaracus

Assyrius, -a, -um, *adj.,*
Assyrian

astringō, -ere, -strinxī,
-strictum, to bind, compress

astrum, -ī, *n.,* star

asȳlum, -ī, *n.,* sanctuary,
asylum

at, *conj.,* but

āter, ātra, ātrum, *adj.,* black,
dark

atque, *conj.,* and

atrox, -ōcis, *adj.,* fierce, cruel,
wild

attendō, -ere, -tendī, -tentum,
to watch, consider

attingō, -ere, -tigī, —, to touch,
reach

attonitus, -a, -um, *adj.,*
thunderstruck, astonished

auctor, -ōris, *m.,* originator,
author, person responsible
for

audeō, -ēre, ausus sum, to dare

auferō, -ferre, abstulī,
ablātum, to carry off,
withdraw, remove

augeō, -ēre, auxī, auctum, to
increase

aura, -ae, *f.,* breeze, wind,
breath

auris, -is, *f.,* ear

aurum, -ī, *n.,* gold

Ausonidae, -ārum, *m.,* Italians

Ausonius, -a, -um, *adj.,*
Ausonian

Auster, -trī, *m.,* the South wind

aut, *conj.,* or

auxilium, -iī, *n.,* help,
assistance

Auernus, -ī, *m.,* Avernus

āuertō, -ere, -uertī, -uersum,
to avert, turn away

axis, axis, *m.,* axle, axis, the
earth's axis, the sky [i.e., the
end of the earth's axis]

Babylōn, -ōnis, *f.,* Babylon

barbarus, -a, -um, *adj.,* foreign,
barbarian

bellum, -ī, *n.,* war

bīgae, -ārum, *f.pl.,* two-horse
chariot

bimaris, -e, *adj.,* between two
seas

bipennis, -is, *f.,* axe with two
blades

birēmis, -is, *f.,* boat with two
banks of oars

brūma, -ae, *f.,* winter

Brūtus, -ī, *m.,* Brutus

bustum, -ī, *n.,* tomb, pyre

cadāuer, -eris, *n.,* body, corpse

cado, -ere, cecidī, cāsum, to
fall, flow

caecus, -a, -um, *adj.,* blind, dark, hidden

caedēs, -is, *f.,* slaughter, bloodshed

caedō, -ere, cecīdī, caesum, to cut down, slaughter

caelicola, -ae, *m.,* heaven-dweller, god

caelum, -ī, *n.,* sky, heaven

Caesar, -aris, *m.,* Caesar

caesariēs, —, *f.,* hair, head of hair, locks

caespes, -itis, *m.,* turf, ground

caesus, -a, -um. *See* caedō

calcō (1), to tread upon, trample

caleō, -ēre, -uī, —, to be warm, glow

campus, -ī, *m.,* plain

Campus Martius, *m.,* the field of Mars, where elections were held at Rome

candeō, -ēre, -uī, —, to glow, be hot

Cannae, -ārum, *f.pl.,* Cannae

canō, -ere, cecinī, cantum, to sing

Canōpus, -ī, *m.,* Canopus

cānus, -a, -um, *adj.,* white

capiō, -ere, cēpī, captum, to take, capture; conceive; contain

Capitōlium, -ī, *n.,* the Capitol

capulus, -ī, *m.,* sword-hilt

caput, -itis, *n.,* head

careō (2) + *abl.,* to lack, be without

carīna, -ae, *f.,* keel, boat

carmen, -inis, *n.,* poem, song, spell

Carrhae, -ārum, *f.pl.,* Carrhae

castra, -ōrum, *n.pl.,* camp

castus, -a, -um, *adj.,* chaste, pure

cāsus, -ūs, *m.,* chance, fortune; disaster, defeat

caterua, -ae, *f.,* squadron

Catō, -ōnis, *m.,* Cato

cauda, -ae, *f.,* tail

causa, -ae, *f.,* cause, reason

cauerna, -ae, *f.,* cavern, cave

cauus, -a, -um, *adj.,* hollow

cēdō, -ere, cessī, cessum, to yield (to), give way + *dat.*

celsus, -a, -um, *adj.,* high, lofty

cernō, -ere, crēuī, —, to see, discern

certē, *adv.,* at least, at any rate

certō (1), to struggle, contend

certus, -a, -um, *adj.,* certain, fixed

ceruix, -īcis, *f.,* neck

cēterus, -a, -um, *adj.,* the rest, remaining

chaos, *n., defective noun,* chaos

cingō, -ere, cinxī, cinctum, to surround, encircle, enclose

cinis, -eris, *m.,* ash

circum, *adv.,* round about, around; *prep.+ acc.,* around

circumeō, -īre, -iī *or* -iuī, -itum, to go around

cīuīlis, -e, *adj.,* civil, of a citizen

cīuis, -is, *m.,* citizen

clādēs, -is, *f.,* disaster, calamity, destruction, carnage

clārus, -a, -um, *adj.,* clear, bright; famous

classis, -is, *f.,* fleet of ships

claudo, -ere, clausī, clausum,
to close, confine, suppress

coeō, -īre, -īuī or -iī, -itum, to
come together, meet

coeptum, -ī, n., usually pl.,
undertaking, enterprise,
plan, scheme

coerceō, -ēre, -cuī, -citum, to
check, restrain

cognātus, -a, -um, adj., related,
kindred

cōgō, cōgere, coēgi, coāctum,
to gather together, force,
compel, compress, restrain

cohors, -rtis, f., cohort, a
subdivision of a legion

colligō, -ere, -lēgī, -lēctum,
to collect, gather up,
concentrate

collis, -is, m., hill

collum, -ī, n., neck

colō, -ere, coluī, cultum, to
worship, venerate; inhabit

colōnus, -ī, m., farmer

color, -ōris, m., color; pretext,
outward show, screen

coma, -ae, f., hair; foliage

comes, -itis, m., companion

comminus, adv., at close
quarters, hand to hand

committō, -mittere, -mīsī,
-missum, to join, bring
together (in battle)

commodō (1), to furnish,
supply, lend

commūnis, -e, adj., shared,
common, general

compāgēs, -is, f., joint,
connection, structure

concīō, -ere, -cīuī, -citus, to stir
up, spur

concordia, -ae, f., harmony,
concord

concors, -cordis, adj., of the
same mind, in unison,
harmonious

concurrō, -ere, -currī,
-cursum, to rush together,
join battle

concutiō, -cutere, -cussī,
-cussum, to shake violently,
shatter, disturb

condō, -ere, -didī, -ditum, to
hide, bury; to found

cōnexus, -a, -um, adj., linked,
joined together

conferō, -ferre, -tulī, -lātum, to
bring together, join, meet

conficiō, -ere, -fēcī, -fectum, to
bring about, accomplish

confine, -is, n., boundary

congerō, -ere, -gessī, -gestum,
to heap up, pile, load

congestus, -ūs, m., heap

coniunx, -iugis, m. and f.,
spouse, husband, wife

conpāgēs, -is, f., joint,
structure, frame

conpellō, -ere, -pulī, -pulsum,
to compel, force

conprendō, -ere, -prendī,
-prensum, to seize, grasp

conscius, -a, -um, adj., having
knowledge of, knowing,
guilty

consentiō, -īre, -sensī,
-sensum, to agree,
acknowledge

consistō, -ere, -stitī, —, to stand, stand still, halt

consors, -sortis, *m. and f.,* consort, partner

consul, -ulis, *m.,* consul

consulō, -ere, consuluī, consultum, + *dat.,* to have regard for, take thought for

consurgō, -ere, consurrexī, consurrectum, to stand up, rise

contineō, -ēre, -tinuī, -tentum, to keep, hold, hold fast

contingō, -ere, -tigī, -tactum, *intransitive,* + *dat.,* to happen, occur

continuō, *adv.,* at once, straightaway

contrā, *prep.* + *acc.,* against, opposite, face to face

contrārius, -a, -um, *adj.,* against, opposed to, confronting

conuertō, -ere, -uertī, -uersum, to turn, direct

Cornēlia, -ae, *f.,* Cornelia

cornū, -ūs, *n.,* horn, crescent

corpus, -oris, *n.,* body

corripiō, -ere, -ripuī, -reptum, to seize, attack, set on fire

corrumpō, -ere, -rūpī, -ruptum, to corrupt, destroy, spoil, mar

corruō, -ere, -ruī, —, to fall, tumble

Crassus, -ī, *m.,* Crassus

crēdō, -ere, -didī, -ditum, + *dat.,* to trust, believe, rely on

crescō, -ere, crēuī, crētum, to grow, increase

crīnis, -is, *m.,* hair

crūdēlis, -e, *adj.,* cruel

cruor, -ōris, *m.,* blood, gore

cubīle, -is, *n.,* bed

cultus, -ūs, *m.,* cultivation, care; smartness; veneration, worship

cum, *conj.,* when, since; *prep.*+ *abl.,* with

cumulus, -ī, *m.,* pile, heap, mound

cunctus, -a, -um, *adj.,* all, entire

cupīdo, -dinis, *f.,* desire, wish, eagerness, greed, lust

cupressus, -ī, *f.,* cypress-tree

cūria, -ae, *f.,* senate-house, senate

currus, -ūs, *m.,* chariot

cursus, -ūs, *m.,* course, path, journey; rapidity, speed

custōdia, -ae, *f.,* guard, control

custōs, -ōdis, *m.,* guard

Cynthia, -ae, *f.,* the goddess of Mount Cynthus, i.e., Diana, the moon

damnō (1), to condemn, doom

damnum, -ī, *n.,* loss, damage, disaster

dē, *prep.* + *abl.,* about, down from

dēbeō (2), to owe, be obliged to

decet, decuit, *impers.,* it is fitting

decōrus, -a, -um, *adj.,* fine, handsome

dēcrētum, -ī, *n.,* decree, declaration

decus, decoris, *n.*, grace, beauty

dēdecus, -oris, *n.*, shame, dishonor, disgrace

dēdiscō, -ere, -didicī, —, to unlearn, forget

dēfōrmis, -e, *adj.*, unsightly, degrading

dēfunctus -a, -um, *adj. and noun,* dead (person)

dēfungor, -fungī, -functus sum, + *abl.*, to have done with, finish

dēgener, -is, *adj.*, contemptible, ignoble

dēmittō, -ere, -mīsī, -missum, to send down, lower, thrust

densus, -a, -um, *adj.*, thick, dense, crowded, packed

dēprecor, dēprecārī, dēprecātus sum, to decline, beg . . . not

dēprendō, -ere, dēprendī, dēprensum, to come upon suddenly, surprise

dēpressus, -a, -um, *adj.*, sunken, low, sloping down

descendō, -ere, descendī, descensum, to descend, go down

dēsertus, -a, -um, *adj.*, deserted, abandoned

dēsiliō, -ere, -siluī, -sultum, to jump down

dēsinō, -ere, -siī, -situm, to cease

dēsum, -esse, -fuī, —, + *dat.*, to fail, be wanting, be lacking

dētrahō, -ere, -traxī, -tractum, to drag down

deus, -ī, *m.*, god

dexter, dextra, dextrum, *adj.*, right

dextra, -ae, *f.*, right hand

dīcō, -ere, dixī, dictum, to say, state

diēs, diēī, *m.*, day, daylight; sky

dīgnus, -a, -um, *adj.*, deserving, worthy

dīlābor, -lābī, -lapsus sum, to melt away, dissolve

dīmitto, -ere, -mīsī, -missum, to let go, resign

dirimō, -ere, -ēmī, -emptum, to part, separate, divide

dīrus, -a, -um, *adj.*, dreadful, terrible, hideous

Dīs, Dītis, *m.*, Dis, god of the Underworld

discernō, -ere, -crēuī, -crētum, to divide, separate

discors, -cordis, *adj.*, discordant, at variance with

discutiō, -cutere, -cussī, -cussum, to break up, shatter, remove, scatter

dispōnō, -pōnere, -posuī, -positum, to distribute, arrange, dispose

disterminō (1), to divide, separate

distraho, -trahere, -trāxī, -tractum, to drag apart

diū, *adv.*, for a long time

dīuellō, -uellere, -uellī, -uulsum *or* -uolsum, to tear apart

dīuidō, -ere, -uīsī, -uīsum, to divide, separate

dō, dare, dedī, datum, to give,
    grant, cause
Dōdōnē, -ēs, *f.,* a town in
    Epirus, seat of an oracle of
    Jupiter
doleō (2), to grieve, suffer,
    resent
dolor, -ōris, *m.,* pain, grief
dominus, -ī, *m.,* master
domitor, -ōris, *m.,* conqueror
domus, -ūs or **-ī,** *f.,* house,
    home
dōnō (1), to give, bestow
dōnum, -ī, *n.,* gift, present
dracō, -ōnis, *m.,* snake
dubitō (1), to hesitate, be in
    doubt
dubius, -a, -um, *adj.,* doubtful,
    hesitating, uncertain, unclear
dūcō, -ere, duxī, ductum, to
    lead
dum, *conj.,* as long as, while,
    until (+ *pres. indicative*),
    provided that (+ *subjunctive*)
dūmēta, -ōrum, *n.pl.,* thorn-
    bushes, thickets
dūmus, -ī, *m.,* thorn-bush,
    bramble
duo, -ae, -o, *adj.,* two
dūrō (1), to endure
dux, ducis, *m.,* leader, general,
    ruler

efficiō, -ere, effēcī, effectum,
    to bring about, make
(effor), -ārī, -ātus, to say, declare
effundō, -ere, -fūdī, -fūsum, to
    pour out, stream, spread
ego, *pron.,* I

ēligo, eligere, ēlēgī, ēlectum, to
    select, choose, pick out
Ēmathia, -ae, *f.,* Emathia
Ēmathius, -a, -um, *adj.,*
    Emathian
ēmicō, -āre, -uī, -ātum, dash
    out, flash (out)
ēn, *interj.,* see!
Erebus, -ī, *m.,* the Underworld,
    the god of darkness
ērigō, -ere, -rexī, -rectum, to
    raise, erect, rouse, stimulate
ēripiō, -ere, -ripuī, -reptum, to
    snatch away
et, *conj.,* and; **et . . . et** both . . .
    and; *adv.,* even
Eurus, -ī, *m.,* the east wind
ēuentus, -ūs, *m.,* fortune, fate
excēdō, -ere, cessī, cessum, to
    go out, leave
excelsus, -a, -um, *adj.,* high, lofty
excipiō, -ere, -cēpī, -ceptum, to
    receive, take up, catch
**excutiō, -cutere, -cussī,
    -cussum,** to shake off, cast
    off, throw away, shoot, expel
exemplum, -ī, *n.,* example
exeō, -īre, -iī, -itum, to go out
exigō, -ere, -ēgī, -actum, to
    drive out, exact
exiguus, -a, -um, *adj.,* small,
    scanty, inadequate, trivial
exiliō, -ere, -uī, —, to leap up,
    spring out
expectō (1), to wait for
expellō, -ere, -pulsī, -pulsum,
    to drive out
**expendō, -ere, expendī,
    expensum,** to weigh

exprimō, -ere, pressī, pressum, to press out, shoot forth

exprōmō, -prōmere, -prompsī, -promptum, to show, reveal

extendō, -tendere, -tendī, -tentum, to stretch out, extend

externus, -a, -um, *adj.,* foreign

extō, extāre, extitī, to stand out, protrude, exist, be found

extrahō, -ere, -traxī, -tractum, to draw out, extract

extrēmus, -a, -um, *adj.,* final, furthest, edge of

extruō, -ere, -uxī, -uctum, to pile up, heap up

exūrō, -ere, -ussī, -ustum, to burn up

exuuiae, -ārum, *f.pl.,* spoils

fābula, -ae, *f.,* story

faciēs, -ēī, *f.,* appearance

facilis, -e, *adj.,* easy

facinus, -oris, *n.,* crime

faciō, -ere, fēcī, factum, to make, do

fāma, -ae, *f.,* fame, reputation, report, rumor

famēs, -is, *f.,* hunger, famine

fās, *defective noun,* right

fateor, -ērī, fassus sum, to grant, acknowledge, say

fātum, -ī, *n.,* fate, destiny, death, destruction

faucēs, -ium, *f.pl.,* throat, jaws

faueō, -ēre, fāuī, fautum, + *dat.,* to favor, support

fauor, -ōris, *m.,* favor, support

fax, facis, *f.,* torch, firebrand

fēlix, -īcis, *adj.,* lucky, fortunate, prosperous

fera, -ae, *f.,* wild beast

fērālis, -e, *adj.,* funereal, deadly, ill-omened, of the dead

feriō, -īre, —, —, to strike

ferō, ferre, tulī, lātum, to carry, bring, lead, bear, endure, report

ferrum, -ī, *n.,* iron, steel; sword

feruidus, -a, -um, *adj.,* burning, fiery

fessus, -a, -um, *adj.,* weary, tired

fibra, -ae, *f.,* fiber, filament; lobe

fidēs, -ēī, *f.,* trust, faith, loyalty, promise, credence, alliance

figūra, -ae, *f.,* figure, form

fingō, -ere, finxī, fictum, to pretend, feign

fīnis, -is, *m.,* boundary, limit, end, stop, finish

fiō, fierī, factus sum, to happen, become, be done

fīrmus, -a, -um, *adj.,* firm, strong

fixus, -a, -um, *adj.,* fixed, immovable

flagellō, -āre, —, —, to whip, lash, scourge

flagrans, -grantis, *adj.,* burning, scorching

flamma, -ae, *f.,* flame, fire, blaze

flātus, -ūs, *m.,* blast

flecto, -ere, flexī, flectum, to turn

flētus, -ūs, *m.,* weeping, lamenting

fluctus, -ūs, *m.,* wave

flūmen, -inis, *n.,* river

fluō, -ere, fluxī, fluctum, to flow, stream, glide

focus, -ī, *adj.,* hearth

foedus, -eris, *n.,* pact, treaty, law

fons, fontis, *m.,* spring, well, source

(for), fārī, fātus sum, *defective verb,* to say, speak

foret = futurus esset

forma, -ae, *f.,* form, beauty

formīdō, -inis, *f.,* fear, terror

forsitan, *adv.,* perhaps, maybe

fortis, -is, -e, *adj.,* strong, brave, courageous

fortūna, -ae, *f.,* fate, fortune, luck, chance, prosperity, success; *sometimes personified as* **Fortūna,** the goddess of luck or chance

foueō, -ēre, fōuī, fōtum, to keep warm, soothe, cherish, support

fragor, -ōris, *m.,* crash

frangō, -ere, frēgī, fractum, to break

frāter, -tris, *m.,* brother

frāternus, -a, -um, *adj.,* brotherly, of a brother

frequentō (1), to visit, attend, occupy

fretum, -ī, *n.,* strait, channel, sea

frīgus, -oris, *n.,* cold

frons, frondis, *f.,* foliage, leaves

frons, frontis, *f.,* brow, forehead, outward appearance

frūgifer, -era, -erum, *adj.,* fruitful, fertile

frustrā, *adv.,* in vain

fuga, -ae, *f.,* flight, escape

fugiō, -ere, fūgī, —, to flee, take flight

fugō (1), to chase away, rout

fulgeō, -ēre, fulsī, to shine, flash, glitter, gleam

fulgur, -ris, *n.,* flash of lightning

fulmen, -inis, *n.,* thunderbolt

fundō, -ere, fūsī, fūsum, to pour, pour out, lay low

fūnestus, -a, -um, *adj.,* deadly, fatal

fūnus, -eris, *n.,* death, funeral

furens, -entis, *adj.,* furious, raging, maddened

furiālis, -e, *adj.,* of the Furies, raging, dreadful, frenzied

furō, -ere, —, —, to rage, rave

furor, -ōris, *m.,* madness, insanity

futūrus, -a, -um, *adj.,* coming, future, imminent

Gallicus, -a, -um, *adj.,* Gallic, of Gaul

Gallus, -ī, *m.,* a Gaul

gaudeō, gaudēre, gāuīsus sum, to enjoy, delight in

gaza, -ae, *f.,* treasure

gelidus, -a, -um, *adj.,* icy, cold

geminō (1), to double

geminus, -a, -um, *adj.,* twin, double, two

gemitus, -ūs, *m.,* groan, sigh

gener, -erī, *m.,* son-in-law
generōsus, -a, -um, *adj.,* noble
gens, gentis, *f.,* clan, family, nation, race
gerō, gerere, gessī, gestum, to wage, conduct, wear
gestō (1), to wear, carry
gigās, -antis, *m.,* giant
glaciālis, -e, *adj.,* icy
gladius, -ī, *m.,* sword
gnātus. *See* **nātus**
gracilis, -e, *adj.,* slender, slight
gradus, -ūs, *m.,* step, pace
Graius, -a, -um, *adj.,* Greek
grāmen, -inis, *n.,* grass
grātus, -a, -um, *adj.,* pleasing, grateful
grauidus, -a, -um, *adj.,* laden, swollen
grauis, -e, *adj.,* heavy; serious
gressus, -ūs, *m.,* step, progress
gurges, -itis, *m.,* whirlpool, flood, water
guttur, -uris, *n.,* throat, breast

habeō (2), to have, hold
habitātor, -ōris, *m.,* inhabitant
habitus, -ūs, *m.,* bearing, appearance
haereō, -ēre, haesī, haesum, to stick, cling
harēna, -ae, *f.,* sand
hasta, -ae, *f.,* spear
haud, *adv.,* not, hardly
hauriō, haurīre, hausī, haustum, to drain
haut. *See* **haud**
Hectoreus, -a, -um, *adj.,* belonging to Hector

Hercēus, -i, *adj.,* Hercean [epithet of Jupiter]
Hēsionē, -ēs, *f.,* Hesione
Hesperia, -ae, *f.,* Italy
Hesperius, -a, -um, *adj.,* Hesperian, western, Italian
heu! *interject.,* oh no!
hīc, *adv.,* here, in this place
hic, haec, hoc, *pron.,* this
hiemps, hiemis, *f.,* winter, storm
hinc, *adv.,* from here, from this place, from this side
hiō (1), to lie open, gape
hirtus, -a, -um, *adj.,* shaggy, rough
honōs, -ōris, *f.,* honor
hōra, -ae, *f.,* hour, season; region
horridus, -a, -um, *adj.,* rough, bristling
horror, -ōris, *m.,* horror, shaking, trembling
hortāmen, -inis, *n.,* encouragement
hostilis, -e, *adj.,* hostile, of the enemy
hostis, -is, *m.,* enemy
hūc, *adv.,* to here, to this place
hūmānus, -a, -um, *adj.,* human
humātor, -ōris, *m.,* person who buries
humus, -ī, *f.,* ground

iaceō, iacēre, iacuī, —, to lie
iam, *adv.,* now, already
ibi, *adv.,* there
(īcō), -ere, īcī, ictum, to strike, hit

ictus, -ūs, *m.,* blow, stroke, thrust

igneus, -a, -um, *adj.,* fiery

ignis, -is, *m.,* fire

ignōrō (1), to be unaware of, not to know

īlex, īlicis, *f.,* holm-oak, ilex-tree

ille, illa, illud, *pron.,* he, she, it; that

illīc, *adv.,* there, in that place

illūc, *adv.,* to that place

imāgō, -inis, *f.,* image, ghost

impellō, -pellere, -pulī, -pulsum, to push, drive, drive on

imperium, -ī, *n.,* command, order, power

impetus, -ūs, *m.,* attack, impulse

īmus, -a, -um, *adj.,* lowest, deepest

in, *prep.* + *abl.,* in, on; in the case of; + *acc.,* into, onto, towards, against, facing, for

inānis, -e, *adj.,* empty, vain

inarātus, -a, -um, *adj.,* unplowed

incendium, -iī, *n.,* fire, conflagration

incertus, -a, -um, *adj.,* uncertain

incola, -ae, *m.* and *f.,* inhabitant

inconsultus, -a, -um, *adj.,* without advice, heedless

incumbō, -ere, incubuī, + *in* + *acc.,* to settle on, lean on, bear down on

incūsō (1), to blame, complain about

inde, *adv.,* from there, from that place, from that side; from then, from that time

indignātus, -a, -um, *adj.,* resentful, reluctant

indignor, indignārī, indignātus sum, to disdain, be resentful of

indomitus, -a, -um, *adj.,* indomitable, untamed

induō, -ere, -uī, -ūtum, to put on, assume, take up

iners, -ertis, *adj.,* sluggish, inert, stagnant

infandus, -a, -um, *adj.,* unspeakable, abominable, inhuman

infēlix, -īcis, *adj.,* unhappy, unlucky, unfortunate

inferō, -ferre, intulī, inlātum, to bring in *or* on

inferus, -a, -um, *adj.,* lower, of the Underworld

infestus, -a, -um, *adj.,* hostile

inficiō, -ere, infēcī, infectum, to stain, dye, taint

informis, -e, *adj.,* shapeless, ugly

infremō, -ere, -uī, to roar

ingemō, -ere, -gemuī, —, to moan, groan, lament

ingens, ingentis, *adj.,* vast, huge

ingerō, -ere, -gessī, -gestum, to heap over, pour in, throw upon, thrust in

inmānis, -e, *adj.,* immense, fierce, savage

inmemor, -oris, *adj.,* unmindful of, forgetful of

inmensus, -a, -um, *adj.,* vast, immeasurable, mighty

inmittō, -ere, inmīsī, inmissum, to send against, throw, direct

inmōbilis, -e, *adj.,* immobile, motionless

inmodicus, -a, -um, *adj.,* immoderate, excessive

innūbō, -ere, -nupsi, -nuptum, to marry into

innumerus, -a, -um, *adj.,* countless

inpār, -aris, *adj.,* + *dat.* unequal, inferior (to)

inpastus, -a, -um, *adj.,* unfed

inpatiens, -entis, *adj.,* + *gen.* intolerant (of), impatient

inpellō, -ere, -pulī, -pulsum, to drive, drive against, shatter

inpendō, -ere, -dī, -sum, to spend, devote

inpius, -a, -um, *adj.,* wicked

inpleō, -ēre, -plēuī, -plētum, to fill, fill up

inplicō, -āre, -āuī, -ātum or **-itum,** to entwine, entangle

inprobus, -a, -um, *adj.,* shameless, presumptuous

inpūrus, -a, -um, *adj.,* unclean, vile

inritus, -a, -um, *adj.,* vain, unfulfilled

inscius, -a, -um, *adj.,* not knowing, unwitting

inserō, -ere, -uī, -ertum, to insert, put into, sink into

insistō, -ere, institī, to stand on + *acc.,* settle on, perch on + *dat. or abl.*

inspīrō (1), to breathe

instar, *n., indecl.,* equal to, as great as

instō, -āre, -stitī, -statum, + *dat.,* to press upon, insist upon

insum, inesse, infuī, to be in, to be on, to be present in

intactus, -a, -um, *adj.,* untouched

intentus, -a, -um, *adj.,* eager, waiting

inter, *prep.* + *acc.,* among, between

intercipiō, -ere, -cēpī, -ceptum, to intercept, snatch, cut off

interpōnō, -ere, -posuī, -positum, to interpose, put between

intus, *adv.,* within

inultus, -a, -um, *adj.,* unavenged, unpunished

inuādō, -ere, -uāsī, -uāsum, to seize

inuehō, -ere, -uexī, -uectum, to carry in, convey

inueniō, -uenīre, -uēni, -uentum, to find

inuideō, -ēre, -uīdī, -uīsum, to refuse, begrudge

inuidia, -ae, *f.,* envy, spite

inuidus, -a, -um, *adj.,* envious

inuigilō (1), to watch over, be awake

inuīsus, -a, -um, *adj.,* hated

inuoluō, -ere, -uoluī, -uolūtum, to wrap up, cover up

Īōnius, -a, -um, *adj.,* Ionian

ipse, -a, -um, *adj.,* himself,
    herself, itself
īra, -ae, *f.,* anger, rage
īrātus, -a, -um, *adj.,* angry
iste, ista, istud, *pron.,* that
Isthmos, -ī, *m.,* the Isthmus of
    Corinth
Ītalia, -ae, *f.,* Italy
iterum, *adv.,* again, a second time
iuba, -ae, *f.,* mane, crest
Iuba, -ae, *m.,* Juba
iubeō, -ēre, iussī, iussum, to
    order
iūdex, -icis, *m.,* judge,
    adjudicator, referee
iūgulō (1), to strangle, murder
iugulum, -ī, *n.,* throat
iugum, -ī, *n.,* yoke, mountain
    ridge
Iūlia, -ae, *f.,* Julia
Iūlius, -a, -um, *adj.,* Julian, of
    the Julian house
iungō, -ere, iūnxī, iūnctum,
    to join
Iuppiter, Iouis, *m.,* Jupiter
iūs, iūris, *n.,* justice, law, right,
    power, legality
iussus, -ūs, *m.,* order
iustē, *adv.,* rightly, justly
iustum, -ī, *n.,* justice
iustus, -a, -um, *adj.,* just
iuuenis, -is, *m.,* young man
iuuō, -āre, iūuī, iūtum, to help,
    assist, please, delight

lābor, lābī, lapsus sum, to slide,
    slip
labor, -ōris, *m.,* work, toil,
    struggle

labōrō (1), to work, strive
lacer, -era, -erum, *adj.,*
    mangled, torn, lacerated
lacerō (1), to lacerate, mangle,
    mutilate
lacertus, -ī, *m.,* arm, upper arm
lacrima, -ae, *f.,* tear
laetus, -a, -um, *adj.,* happy,
    prosperous
lampas, -adis, *f.,* torch
lancea, -ae, *f.,* lance, spear
langueō, -ēre, —, —, to droop,
    be faint
languidus, -a, -um, *adj.,* faint,
    weak, weary
languor, -ōris, *m.,* weakness,
    exhaustion
lapsus, -ūs, *m.,* fall, collapse
laqueus, -ī, *m.,* noose, rope
lar, laris, *m.,* household god
lassus, -a, -um, *adj.,* tired,
    weary
lātē, *adv.,* far and wide,
    extensively
latebra, -ae, *f.,* hiding-place
lateō, -ēre, -uī, —, to be
    concealed, lie hidden
Latiāris, -e, *adj.,* Latian, of
    Latium
Latium, -ī, *n.,* Latium
Latius, -a, -um, *adj.,* Latian, of
    Latium
lātus, -a, -um, *adj.,* wide, broad
laurea, -ae, *f.,* crown of laurel,
    bay-wreath
laus, laudis, *f.,* praise
Lāuīnius, -a, -um, *adj.,* of
    Lavinium
laxō (1), to open, widen

legō, -ere, lēgī, lectum, to read
leō, -ōnis, *m.*, lion
Lesbos, -ī, *f.*, Lesbos
Lēthaeus, -a, -um, *adj.*, of Lethe
lētifer, -a, -um, *adj.*, deadly, fatal
lētum, -ī, *n.*, death
Leucas, -adis, *f.*, Leucas
leuis, -e, *adj.*, light, swift, nimble, light-armed
leuō (1), to lift, support
lex, lēgis, *f.*, law
lībertās, -ātis, *f.*, liberty, freedom
lībrō (1), to hold suspended, balance, poise
Libycus, -a, -um, *adj.*, Libyan
Libyē, -ēs, *f.*, Libya, Africa
licentia, -ae, *adj.*, freedom, liberty, lack of restraint
licet, licuit, *impers.*, it is allowed
līmes, -itis, *m.*, boundary, limit
lītus, -oris, *n.*, shore
locō (1), to place
locus, -ī, *m.*, place, position
longē, *adv.*, far
longus, -a, -um, *adj.*, long
loquor, loquī, locūtus sum, to speak, talk, say
lūceō, -ēre, luxī, —, to shine
luctus, -ūs, *m.*, grief, sorrow
lūcus, -ī, *m.*, grove, sacred grove
lūgeō, -ēre, luxī, luctum, to grieve, mourn
lūmen, -inis, *n.*, light, eye
lupus, -ī, *m.*, wolf

lustra, -orum, *n.pl.*, haunts of wild beasts, impenetrable country
lustrō (1), to purify, sanctify; scan, consider, survey
lux, lūcis, *f.*, light, day; life
lūxus, -ūs, *m.*, luxury
lymphātus, -a, -um, *adj.*, frantic, crazy

māchina, -ae, *f.*, device, mechanism
maculō (1), to stain, pollute
madeō, -ēre, -uī, —, to be wet, drip
madidus, -a, -um, *adj.*, wet, moist
maestus, -a, -um, *adj.*, unhappy, grieving, gloomy, dismal
magis, *adv.*, more
magister, -trī, *m.*, master, ship's captain
magnus, -a, -um, *adj.*, great, big
Magnus, -ī, *m.*, Magnus, Pompey
māiestās, -ātis, *f.*, dignity
māiores, -um, *m.pl.*, ancestors
mala, -ōrum, *n.pl.*, troubles, hardships
male, *adv.*, badly, evilly
malīgnus, -a, -um, *adj.*, evil, hostile
malus, -a, -um, *adj.*, bad, evil
mālus, -ī, *m.*, mast
mandō (1), to entrust, assign
maneō, -ēre, mansī, mansum, to stay, remain
mānēs, -ium, *m.pl.*, spirits of the dead, ghosts, shades

manus, -ūs, *f.,* hand; band of
men

marceō, -ēre, —, —, to droop,
be languid, wither

mare, -is, *n.,* sea

marītus, -ī, *m.,* husband

Marius, -ī, *m.,* Marius

Mars, Martis, *m.,* Mars, god of
War

māteria, -ae, *f.,* material,
substance, solid matter

mātūrus, -a, -um, *adj.,* ripe,
early

Maurus, -ī, *m.,* Moor

medium, -iī, *n.,* the middle
part, the midst, the common
stock

medius, -a, -um, *adj.,* middle,
middle of, in the middle

medulla, -ae, *f.,* marrow,
innards

membrum, -ī, *n.,* limb,
member

meminī, -isse, —, *defective
verb,* to remember

memorābilis, -e, *adj.,*
memorable

Memphis, -idis, *f.,* Memphis

mens, mentis, *f.,* mind, thought

mereō, -ēre, -uī, -itum, to
deserve, earn

mergō, -ere, mersī, mersum, to
plunge, sink

meritus, -a, -um, *adj.,*
deserved, fit

merx, mercis, *f.,* goods,
merchandise, reward

metallum, -ī, *n.,* metal

metuō, -ere, -uī, —, to fear

meus, -a, -um, *poss. pron.,* my,
mine

mīles, -itis, *m.,* soldier

minor, minarī, minātus sum,
to threaten

mīrātor, -ōris, *m.,* admirer

mīror, mīrārī, mīratus sum, to
admire, be amazed at, hold
in awe

misceō, -ēre, miscuī, mixtum,
to mix, mingle, combine

miser, -era, -erum, *adj.,*
wretched, poor

miserandus, -a, -um, *adj.,*
pitiable, lamentable

mītis, -e, *adj.,* soft, kind, gentle

mittō, mittere, mīsī, missum,
to send, throw

modicus, -a, -um, *adj.,*
moderate, modest, small

modo, *adv.,* only

modus, -ī, *m.,* way; limit

moenia, -ium, *n.pl.,* walls, city
walls

mollis, -e, *adj.,* soft, easy,
yielding, effeminate

mons, montis, *m.,* hill,
mountain

monstrātor, -ōris, *m.,* guide

monstrō (1), to show

monstrum, -ī, *n.,* portent,
omen, abomination

mora, -ae, *f.,* delay, stay,
impediment, obstacle

morior, morī, mortuus sum,
to die

mors, -tis, *f.,* death

mortālis, -e, *adj.,* mortal

mōs, mōris, *m.,* custom, habit

motus, -ūs, *m.,* movement, upheaval

moueō, -ēre, mōuī, mōtum, to move, sway, set in motion

mox, *adv.,* soon

mūcrō, -ōnis, *m.,* sword-point

mūgiō, -īre, mūgīuī, mūgītum, to roar, rumble, bellow

multum, *adv.,* much, very

multus, -a, -um, *adj.,* much, many

Munda, -ae, *f.,* Munda [a city in Spain]

mundus, -ī, *m.,* sky, world, universe

murmur, -ris, *n.,* murmur, roar, growling

mūrus, -ī, *m.,* wall

Mūsae, -ārum, *f.pl.,* the Muses

Mutina, -ae, *f.,* Mutina

mūtō (1), to change

Nāis, —, *f. defective noun,* Naiad, water-nymph

nam, *conj.,* for, because

nascor, nasci, nātus sum, to be born

natō (1), to swim, be drenched

Nātūra, -ae, *f.,* Nature

nātus, -ī, *m.,* son

naufragium, -iī, *n.,* shipwreck

nāuita, -ae, *m.,* sailor

nē, *conj.,* lest, so that not

-ne, *particle, indicating a question*

nec, neque, *conj.,* nor, and not; **nec . . . nec,** neither . . . nor

nefandus, -a, -um, *adj.,* unspeakable, abominable

nefās, *n., indecl.,* impious deed, crime, guilt, abomination

negō (1), to deny, say . . . not

nemus, -oris, *n.,* grove, wood, forest

nepōs, -ōtis, *m.,* grandson, descendant

nēquīquam, *adv.,* in vain

nēquis = nē, *conj.,* + **quis,** *pron., adj.,* lest anyone, any

Nerō, -ōnis, *m.,* Nero

neruus, -ī, *m.,* sinew, tendon, muscle

nesciō, -īre, -īuī, —, not to know

nescius, -a, -um, *adj.,* unaware, not knowing how to

niger, nigra, nigrum, *adj.,* dark, black

nihil, *n., indecl.,* nothing

nil, *n., indecl. See* **nihil**

Nīlus, -ī, *m.,* the river Nile

nimius, -a, -um, *adj.,* too much, too great, excessive

nisi, *conj.,* unless, except, if not

nōbilis, -e, *adj.,* noble, renowned

nocens, -entis, *adj.,* harmful, wicked, guilty

nocturnus, -a, -um, *adj.,* nocturnal, nighttime

nōdōsus, -a, -um, *adj.,* knotty

nōlō, nōlle, nōluī, —, to be unwilling, not to want

nōmen, -inis, *n.,* name

nōn, *adv.,* not

nōndum, *adv.,* not yet

noscō, -ere, nōuī, nōtum, to know, recognize

noster, -stra, -strum, *poss.
pron.*, our, Roman
nōtus, -a, -um, *adj.*, well-
known, familiar
nouus, -a, -um, *adj.*, new,
recent
nox, noctis, *f.*, night
noxius, -a, -um, *adj.*, harmful,
guilty
nūbēs, -is, *f.*, cloud
nūbila, -ōrum, *n.pl.*, clouds,
rain clouds
nūdō (1), to strip bare, uncover,
expose
nūdus, -a, -um, *adj.*, naked, bare
nullus, -a, -um, *adj.*, no, none
nūmen, -inis, *n.*, (divine) power
numerō (1), to count
numquam, *adv.*, never
nunc, *adv.*, now
nūtō (1), to nod, totter
Nympha, -ae, *f.*, nymph, semi-
divine spirit of nature

ō! *interj.*, oh!
obeō, -īre, -īuī, -itum, to die
oblīquus, -a, -um, *adj.*, slanting
oblīuia, -ōrum, *n.pl.*,
forgetfulness, oblivion
obruō, -ere, obruī, obrutum, to
overwhelm, crush
obscūrō (1), to obscure,
overshadow
obscūrus, -a, -um, *adj.*, dark,
shady, murky, obscure
obsequor, -sequī, -secūtus
sum, to comply, obey
obstō, -āre, -stetī, —, to
obstruct, stand in the way

obuius, -a, -um, *adj.*, meeting,
facing, opposing
occupō (1), to seize, grab
Oetaeus, -a, -um, *adj.*, of Mt.
Oeta
offerō, -ferre, obtulī, oblātum,
to offer, bring to
ōlim, *adv.*, once, long ago
ōmen, -inis, *n.*, omen, sign,
portent
omnis, -e, *adj.*, every, all
opācō (1), to make shady, shade
opera, -ae, *f.*, work, effort,
support
opes, opum, *f.pl.*, riches,
wealth
oppōnō, -ere, -posuī, -positum,
to set before, draw up
opus, -eris, *n.*, work, task
ōra, ōrae, *f.*, region, border
orbis, -is, *m.*, circle, ring, orbit,
world
ordō, -dinis, *m.*, rank, order
Orestēs, -is, *m.*, Orestes
ornus, -ī, *f.*, ash-tree
ōrō (1), to beg, pray
ōs, ōris, *n.*, face, mouth
os, ossis, *n.*, bone

paelex, -icis, *f.*, mistress,
paramour
Pallas, -adis, *f.*, Pallas, Athene
pallens, -entis, *adj.*, faint, pale
pallidus, -a, -um, *adj.*, pale,
colorless
pallor, pallōris, *m.*, paleness,
pallor
palma, -ae, *f.*, palm, hand
Pān, Pānos, *m.*, Pan, pl. *Pānēs*

pār, paris, *adj. or noun,* equal, like, a match

Parcae, -ārum, *f.pl.,* the Fates

parcō, -ere, pepercī, parsum, + *dat. or infinitive,* to spare, refrain from

parens, -entis, *m.* and *f.,* parent

pāreō, -ēre, -uī, —, + *dat.,* to obey

parō (1), to prepare, obtain, get, win

pars, partis, *f.,* part, role, element

Parthicus, -a, -um, *adj.,* Parthian

parum, *adv.,* too little

paruus, -a, -um, *adj.,* small, little

pateō, -ēre, -uī, —, to lie open, be open

pater, -tris, *m.,* father; senator

patiens, -ientis, *adj.,* patient, enduring

patior, patī, passus sum, to suffer, endure, allow

patria, -ae, *f.,* fatherland, native land

patricius, -a, -um, *adj.,* patrician

patrius, -a, -um, *adj.,* ancestral

paueō, -ēre, pāuī, —, to fear, tremble at, quake with fear

pauor, -ōris, *m.,* fear, panic

pax, -ācis, *f.,* peace

pectus, -oris, *n.,* breast, chest, heart

pelagus, -ī, *m.,* sea

Pellaeus, -a, -um, *adj.,* of Pella

pellō, -ere, pepulī, pulsum, to drive away, dispel

Pelopēus, -a, -um, *adj.,* of Pelops, son/descendant of Pelops

Pēlūsiacus, -a, -um, *adj.,* of Pelusium

penātēs, -ium, *m.pl.,* household gods

pendeo, -ēre, pependī, —, to hang, hang in the balance, totter

penitus, *adv.,* deeply

Pentheus, -eī, *m.,* Pentheus

per, *prep.* + *acc.,* through, along, during, by means of, for, by

percellō, -ere, -culī, -culsum, to strike, hit, upset

percutiō, -ere, -cussī, -cussum, to strike, affect

perdō, -ere, -didī, -ditum, to lose, destroy

peremptus. *See* **perimo**

pereō, -īre, -iī, -itum, to die, perish, be ruined

pererrō (1), to wander

perfodiō, -ere, -fōdī, -fossum, to pierce, stab

Pergama, -ōrum, *n.pl.,* Pergamum, the citadel of Troy

perimō, -ere, -ēmī, -emptum, to destroy, kill, murder

permaneō, -ēre, -mansī, -mansum, to endure, last

permisceō, -ēre, -miscuī, -mixtum, to mix up, throw into confusion, mingle

permittō, -ere, -mīsī, -missum, to let, permit, grant, allow

perrumpō, -ere, -rūpī, -ruptum, to break through, split

persequor, -sequī, -secūtus sum, to pursue, follow after

Perusīnus, -a, -um, *adj.,* belonging to Perusia [modern Perugia]

peruius, -a, -um, *adj.,* passable

petītor, -ōris, *m.,* seeker

petō, -ere, -īuī, -ītum, to seek, ask, make for, aim at

Pharius, -a, -um, *adj.,* of Pharos

Pharsālia, -ae, *f.,* Pharsalia

Pharsālicus, -a, -um, *adj.,* of Pharsalia

Phoēbē, -ēs, *f.,* the goddess Diana, sister of Phoebus Apollo

Phoebēus, -a, -um, *adj.,* of Phoebus, of Apollo

Phoebus, -ī, *m.,* Phoebus, Apollo, the sun(-god)

Phrygius, -a, -um, *adj.,* Phrygian, Trojan

Phryx, -ygis, *adj.,* Phrygian

pietās, -ātis, *f.,* dutiful behavior, devotion

pīgnus, -oris, *n.,* pledge, bond

pīlum, -ī, *n.,* javelin

Pindus, -ī, *m.,* Mt. Pindus

pīrāticus, -a, -um, *adj.,* of the pirates

pīus, -a, -um, *adj.,* good, holy

placeō (2) + *dat.,* to please

placidus, -a, -um, *adj.,* kindly, calm, tranquil

plācō (1), + *dat.,* to be favorably disposed, reconciled (with)

plausus, -ūs, *m.,* applause

plēbēius, -a, -um, *adj.,* of the common people, common, ordinary

plēbēs, plēbēī, *f.,* the plebs, the people, the masses

plēnus, -a, -um, *adj.,* full

plūrimus, -a, -um, *adj.,* most numerous, very many

plūs, plūris, *adj.,* more

pluuiālis, -e, *adj.,* rainy

poena, -ae, *f.,* punishment

Poenus, -a, -um, *adj.,* Carthaginian

Pompēius, -ī, *m.,* Pompey

pondus, -eris, *n.,* weight, mass

pōnō, -ere, posuī, positum, to put, put down, put aside, place

Ponticus, -a, -um, *adj.,* Pontic

pontus, -ī, *m.,* sea

Pontus, -ī, *m.,* the Black Sea

populāris, -e, *adj.,* popular, of the people

populus, -ī, *m.,* people, race

portitor, -ōris, *m.,* ferryman

poscō, -ere, poposcī, —, to demand

possideō, -ēre, -sēdī, -sessum, to own, possess

possum, posse, potuī, — , to be able

post, *prep.* + *acc.,* after

posteritās, -ātis, *f.,* posterity

postquam, *conj.,* after

potens, -entis, *adj.* + *gen.,* able, powerful (over)

potestās, -ātis, *f.,* power

praebeō (2), to offer, show, provide

praecēdō, -ere, -cessī, -cessum, to precede, outstrip

praeceps, *adv.,* headlong

praeceps, -cipitis, *adj.,* headlong, in haste

praeceps, -cipitis, *n.,* a sheer drop, a precipitous descent

praeda, -ae, *f.,* loot, plunder

praeferō, -ferre, -tulī, -lātum, to put before, prefer

praeparō (1), to prepare

praesāgium, -ī, *n.,* presentiment, foreboding

praestō, -āre, -itī, -itum, to show, present

praestringō, -ere, -strinxī, -strictum, to dazzle, confuse

precor, precārī, precātus sum, to pray, beg

premō, premere, pressī, pressum, to press upon, overwhelm, confine

pretium, -ī, *n.,* price, prize

prīmum, *adv.,* first

prīmus, -a, -um, *adj.,* first, uttermost, extreme, the first part of, earliest, best

prior, -ōris, *adj.,* former, prior, previous, ahead

prīuatus, -ī, *m.,* someone who holds no public office

pro, *interj.,* oh!

prōbō (1), to approve, prove, test

procul, *adv.,* far from

prōcumbō, -ere, -cubuī, -cubitum, to fall forward, down

proelium, -iī, *n.,* battle, fight

profānus, -a, -um, *adj.,* profane, unclean

prōiciō, -ere, -iēcī, -iectum, to cast out, throw out

prōmittō, -ere, -mīsī, -missum, to promise

prōnus, -a, -um, *adj.,* leaning forward, drooping

prōpellō, -ere, -pulī, -pulsum, to push over, drive on

properē, *adv.,* fast, swiftly

properō (1), to hurry, hasten

propior, -ius, *adj.,* closer, nearer

prōrumpō, -ere, -rūpī, -ruptum, to break out, rush forth

proscindō, -ere, proscindī, proscissum, to cut the surface of, gash

prosperus, -a, -um, *adj.,* fortunate, successful

prospiciō, -ere, -spexī, -spectum, to look at, survey

prosternō, -ere, -strāuī, -strātum, to lay low, overthrow

prosum, prodesse, profuī, —, + *dat.* to benefit, profit

prōtinus, *adv.,* at once

proximus, -a, -um, *adj.,* the nearest, next

Ptolemaeus, -ī, *m.,* Ptolemy

pudet, puduit, *impers.,* it shames, I am ashamed

pudor, -ōris, *m.,* shame

puer, -ī, *m.,* boy

pugna, -ae, *f.,* fight, battle

pugnō (1), to fight

pulmō, -ōnis, *m.,* lung

pulsō (1), to strike, impel
puluis, -eris, *n.,* dust
pūniceus, -a, -um, *adj.,* red, ruddy
puppis, -is, *f.,* ship, stern
purgō (1), to purify
pūrus, -a, -um, *adj.,* pure
puter, -tris, -tre, *adj.,* rotten, decaying
putō (1), to think
Pyrrhus, -ī, *m.,* Pyrrhus

quā, *adv.,* where
quaerō, -ere, -sīuī, -sītum, to seek, ask, question
quālis, -e, *adj.,* of what kind; of such a kind, like, as
quāliter, *adv.,* as, just as
quam, *adv.,* how; than
quamuīs, *conj.,* although
quantum, *adv.,* as much as, to as great an extent
quantus, -a, -um, *adj.,* how great
quatiō, -ere, —, quassum, to shake
-que, *conj.,* and
-que . . . -que, *conj.,* both . . . and
quercus, -ūs, *f.,* oak tree
querella, -ae, *f.,* lament
queror, querī, questus sum, to complain, lament
quī, quae, quod, *pron.,* who, what, which?; *adj.,* any
quīcumque, quaecumque, quodcumque, *pron.* whoever, whatever
quiēs, -ētis, *f.,* quiet, rest

quippe, *conj.,* the fact is, indeed
Quirīnus, -ī, *m.,* Quirinus, name given to the deified Romulus
quid? *adv.,* why?
quis, quid? *pron., adj.,* who, what?
quisquam, quicquam, *indef. pron.,* anyone, anybody
quisque, quaeque, quidque, *indef. pron.,* each, each one, each person
quisquis, quidquid, *indef. pron.,* whoever, whatever
quō, *adv.* and *conj.,* where, to what place, to the place where
quod, *conj.,* because; the fact that
quod si, *conj.,* but if
quōquam, *adv.,* to anywhere
quoque, *conj.,* also, too

rādix, -īcis, *f.,* root
rāmus, -ī, *m.,* branch
rapiō, -ere, rapuī, raptum, to snatch, seize, grab
rārus, -a, -um, *adj.,* rare, scattered, occasional
ratis, -is, *f.,* ship, boat
recēdō, -cēdere, -cessī, -cessum, to go back, recede, be separated from
receptō (1), to take back, receive, admit
recīdō, -ere, -cīdī, -cīsum, to cut off
recipiō, -ere, -cēpī, -ceptum, to receive, admit

recollīgō, -ere, -lēgī, -lectum, to gather again, collect

rector, -ōris, *m.,* ruler

recumbo, -ere, recubuī, to lie, lie at rest

reddō, -ere, reddidī, redditum, to give back, restore

redeō, -īre, rediī, reditum, to go back, return, recur, recoil upon

rēfert, rēferre, rettulit, *impers. verb,* it makes a difference, it is important

refugiō, -ere, -fūgī, —, to shun, flee away from

rēgia, -ae, *f.,* palace

rēgius, -a, -um, *adj.,* royal, belonging to the king

regnō (1), to rule

regnum, -ī, *n.,* kingdom, tyranny, rule, power

relinquō, -ere, relīquī, relictum, to leave, abandon

remaneō, -ēre, -mansi, —, to stay behind, remain

remitto, -ere, -mīsī, -missum, to send back, ease, let up

remoueō, -ēre, -mōuī, -mōtum, to remove

rēmus, -ī, *m.,* oar

reor, rērī, ratus sum, to think

reparō (1), to restore, repair

repellō, -ere, -pulsī, -pulsum, to drive back

repetō, -petere, -petīuī, -petītum, to seek again, revert to

rēs, reī, *f.,* thing, matter, event, affair; *pl.* situation

resideō, -ēre, -sēdī, —, to reside, be seated

resoluō, -ere, -soluī, -solūtum, to unfasten, melt

respiciō, -ere, -spexī, -spectum, to look back at, heed, have respect for

restituō, -ere, -stituī, -stitūtum, to restore

retegō, -ere, -texī, -tectum, to uncover, reveal

retineō, -ēre, -tinuī, -tentum, to keep back, restrain

reuellō, -ere, -uellī, -uolsum *or* **-uulsum,** to pull away, tear out

reuerentia, -ae, *f.,* respect

reuertor, reuertī, reuersus sum, to turn back, return

reuocō (1), to recall, call back, summon back

rex, rēgis, *m.,* king

Rhoetēum, -ī, *n.,* Rhoeteum

rigens, -entis, *adj.,* stiff, frozen

rigescō, -ere, -guī, to grow stiff

rigidus, -a, -um, *adj.,* stiff, hard

rīpa, -ae, *f.,* river bank

rīte, *adv.,* solemnly, with due observance

rītus, -ūs, *m.,* rite, ritual, custom

rīuus, -ī, *m.,* stream

rōbur, -oris, *n.,* oak tree, tree-trunk, hard timber; strength

rogus, -ī, *m.,* funeral pyre

Rōma, -ae, *f.,* Rome

Rōmānus, -a, -um, *adj.,* Roman

rostra, -ōrum, *n.pl.,* the platform from which speakers addressed the Roman people

rōtō (1), to whirl about, send rolling

Rubicō, -ōnis, *m.,* the river Rubicon

ruīna, -ae, *f.,* ruin, collapse, destruction

rumpō, -ere, rūpī, ruptum, to break

ruō, -ere, ruī, rutum, to rush, fall in ruin, collapse

rūpēs, -is, *f.,* rock, cliff

rūricola, -ae, *m., f.,* country-dweller, rustic

rūs, rūris, *n.,* fields, countryside

Sabīnus, -a, -um, *adj.,* Sabine

sacer, -cra, -crum, *adj.,* sacred; *n.pl.,* sacred rites, ceremonies

sacerdōs, -ōtis, *m.,* priest

sacrō (1), to dedicate, consecrate

saeculum, -ī, *n.,* age, generation, century

saepe, *adv.,* often

saeuus, -a, -um, *adj.,* savage, wild

salūtō (1), to greet

saluus, -a, -um, *adj.,* unharmed, preserved, maintained

sanguis, -guinis, *m.,* blood

satelles, -itis, *m.,* attendant, minion

satiō (1), to satiate, glut

satis, *adv.,* enough, sufficiently

saturō (1), to fill, glut

saxum, -ī, *n.,* rock, stone

scelerātus, -a, -um, *adj.,* wicked

scelus, -eris, *n.,* crime, evil deed

sceptrum, -ī, *n.,* scepter

scindō, -ere, scidī, scissum, to rip, tear

sciō, -īre, -īuī, -ītum, to know, know how to

scopulus, -ī, *m.,* rock, cliff

scrūtor, scrūtārī, scrūtātus sum, to search, examine

Scythicus, -a, -um, *adj.,* Scythian

sē, *reflex. pron.,* himself, herself, itself, themselves

secō, -āre, -uī, -ctum, to cut, cut off

sēcrētum, -ī, *n.,* secret, mystery

secundus, -a, -um, *adj.,* following, favorable

secūris, -is, *f.,* axe

sēcūrus, -a, -um, *adj.,* untroubled, ignoring; + *gen.,* oblivious (of), indifferent (to)

sed, *conj.,* but

sedeō, -ēre, sēdī, sessum, to sit, sink, settle

sēdēs, -is, *m.,* seat, abode, home

sēmianimis, -e, *adj.,* half-alive

sēmirutus, -a, -um, *adj.,* half-destroyed

sēmiuir, -uirī, *m.,* half-man, eunuch

semper, *adv.,* always

senātus, -ūs, *m.,* Senate

senex, senis, *m.,* old man

senium, -ī, *n.,* old age

sentiō, -īre, sensī, sensum, to feel, realize

sēparō (1), to divide, separate

Septimius, -ī, *m.,* Septimius

sepulchrum, -ī, *n.,* tomb, grave

sequor, sequī, secūtus sum, to follow, pursue, chase

Sērēs, -um, *m.pl.,* Seres [a people, living in what today is China]

seriēs, *f. defective noun,* series, chain

serpō, -ere, serpsī, serptum, to creep, crawl, snake

seruīlis, -e, *adj.,* servile, of a slave

seruiō (4) + *dat.,* to serve

seruō (1), to keep, keep safe, preserve

set. *See* **sed**

sī, *conj.,* if

sībila, -ōrum, *n.pl.,* hissing

sīc, *adv.,* thus, in this way, so

sīcut, *adv.,* just as

sīdō, -ere, —, —, to sink, settle

sīdus, -eris, *n.,* star

Sīgēus, -a, -um, *adj.,* of Sigeum

signum, -ī, *n.,* sign, standard; constellation

silens, -tis, *adj.,* silent, *pl.* the dead

silua, -ae, *f.,* wood, forest, *pl.* trees

Siluānus, -ī, *m.,* Silvanus, a Roman god

Simoīs, -entis, *m.,* Simois

simul, *adv.,* at the same time

simulācrum, -ī, *n.,* likeness, image, statue

sine, *prep.* + *abl.,* without

singulī, -ae, -a, *adj.,* single, individual

singultus, -ūs, *m.,* sob

sinus, -ūs, *m.,* fold, hollow, embrace, breast

siquis = sī, *conj.,* + **quis,** *pron.,* if any, if anyone

situs, -ūs, *m.,* neglect, decay

socer, -erī, *m.,* father-in-law

socius, -iī, *m.,* companion, ally, associate

sōl, sōlis, *m.,* the sun, *pl.* sunlight

sōlācium, -ī, *n.,* consolation

sōlum, *adv.,* only

solum, -ī, *n.,* soil, ground

sōlus, -a, -um, *adj.,* only, sole, lonely

soluō, -ere, soluī, solūtum, to loosen, free, unleash, break, disintegrate

somnus, -ī, *m.,* sleep

sonipēs, -pedis, *m.,* horse, charger, steed

sonitus, -ūs, *m.,* sound, noise

sonō, -āre, sonuī, sonitum, to make a noise, resound, crash

sopor, -ōris, *m.,* sleep, slumber

sopōrifer, -era, -erum, *adj.,* sleepy, drowsy

sors, sortis, *f.,* lot

spargō, -ere, sparsī, sparsum, to sprinkle, scatter, break up

spectāculum, -ī, *n.,* show, sight

spectō (1), to look at

speculor, speculārī, speculātus sum, to consider, observe

spēs, -eī, *f.,* hope

spīrō (1), to breathe

spoliō (1), to plunder, strip

sponte, *abl. s. of* **spōns,** *f.,* willingly, freely, of one's own accord

squāleō, -ēre, -uī, —, to be rough, barren, murky

stāmen, -inis, *n.,* thread

statuō, -ere, -uī, -ūtum, to decide

sterilis, -e, *adj.,* barren, unfruitful

sternō, -ere, strāuī, strātum, to spread, lay low, prostrate

stimulō (1), to goad, spur on

stimulus, -ī, *m.,* goad, spur, incentive

stō, stāre, stetī, statum, to stand

strāgēs, -is, *f.,* ruin, destruction, slaughter

stringō, -ere, strinxī, strictum, to draw, unsheathe a sword

struō, -ere, struxī, structum, to arrange, furnish, build, devise

Stygius, -a, -um, *adj.,* Stygian

Styx, Stygis, *f.,* the river Styx

sub, *prep. + acc. or abl.,* under

subdūcō, -ere, -duxī, -ductum, to take away

subeō, -īre, -iī, -itum, to go under, enter, pierce

subigō, -ere, -ēgī, -actum, to conquer, overcome

subitus, -a, -um, *adj.,* sudden

sublātus, -a, -um. *See* **tollō**

sublīmis, -e, *adj.,* high, tall, lofty

submissus, -a, -um, *adj.,* low, humble, groveling

subsīdō, -ere, -sēdī, -sessum, to sink down, settle, crouch

subuertō, -ere, subuertī, subuersum, to overturn, destroy, ruin

succēdō, -ere, -cessī, -cessum, to go up, move into

succendō, -ere, -cendī, -censum, to light, set on fire

successus, -ūs, *m.,* success

sufficiō, -ere, suffēcī, suffectum, + *dat.,* to have the strength for, to have the capacity for

suffīgō, -ere, suffixī, suffixum, to fasten, attach

Sulla, -ae, *m.,* Sulla

sum, esse, fuī, —, to be

summoueō, -mouēre, -mōuī, -mōtum, to remove, keep away

summus, -a, -um, *adj.,* very high, highest, greatest, last

sūmō, -ere, sumpsī, sumptum, to take, take up

supera, -ōrum, *n.pl.,* the world above

superbus, -a, -um, *adj.,* proud

superī, -ōrum, *m.pl.,* the gods

superō (1), to go over, rise above, surmount, defeat, cross

superstes, -itis, *adj.,* surviving

supersum, -esse, -fuī, —, to remain

suprā, *prep.+ acc.,* above, over

suprēmus, -a, -um, *adj.,* highest, last, final

surdus, -a, -um, *adj.,* deaf

surgō, -ere, surrexī, —, to rise

suspiciō, -ere, -spexī, -spectum, to look up at

sustineō, -ēre, -tinuī, -tentum,
to support, sustain, persist

suus, -a, -um, *poss. pron.*, his,
her, its, their [own]

Syrtes, -ium, *f.pl.*, the Syrtes,
sandbanks off the coast of
Africa

tābēs, -is, *f.*, decay, putrefaction

taceō (2), to be silent

taeda, -ae, *f.*, torch, marriage
torch

Taenarius, -a, -um, *adj.*, of
Taenarus

tālis, -e, *adj.*, such, of such a
kind

tam, *adv.*, so, so much

tamen, *adv.*, however,
nevertheless

tandem, *adv.*, finally, at last

tangō, -ere, tetigī, tactum, to
touch

tantum, *adv.*, only, to such an
extent, so much

tantus, -a, -um, *adj.*, so great,
so much

Tarpēius, -a, -um, *adj.*, Tarpeian

Tartara, -ōrum, *n.pl.*, Tartarus

Tartareus, -a, -um, *adj.*, of
Tartarus

taxus, -ī, *f.*, yew tree

tectum, -ī, *n.*, roof, house

tegō, -ere, texī, tectum, to
cover

tellūs, -ūris, *f.*, land, ground

tēlum, -ī, *n.*, weapon, spear

temerārius, -a, -um, *adj.*, rash,
reckless

temerō (1), to violate, profane,
defile, desecrate

templum, -ī, *n.*, temple,
precinct

temptō (1), to try, attempt

tempus, -oris, *n.*, time

tendō, -ere, tetendī, tentum, to
stretch, head to, march to

tenebrae, -ārum, *f.pl.*, darkness

teneō, tenēre, tenuī, —, to hold,
keep, occupy

tentōrium, -ī, *n.*, tent

tepidus, -a, -um, *adj.*, warm

ter, *adv.*, three times

tergum, -ī, *n.*, back

terminus, -ī, *m.*, end, term,
limit

terra, -ae, *f.*, land, ground,
country

terreō (2), to terrify, frighten

terror, -ōris, *m.*, terror, alarm

tertius, -a, -um, *adj.*, third

testor, -ārī, testātus, to attest,
be a witness, give evidence
of

thalamus, -ī, *m.*, marriage-
chamber

theātrum, -ī, *n.*, theater

Thessalia, -ae, *f.*, Thessaly

Thessalicus, -a, -um, *adj.*,
Thessalian

Thessalus or Thessalius -a,
-um, *adj.*, Thessalian

timeō, -ēre, -uī, —, to fear, be
afraid

timor, -ōris, *m.*, fear

Tītān, -ānos, *m.*, Titan, the
sun-god

toga, -ae, *f.*, toga, peacetime

tollō, -ere, sustulī, sublātum,
to lift, raise, remove, destroy

Tonans, -antis, *m.,* the Thunderer, Jupiter

tonō, -āre, -uī, —, to thunder, roar

torpor, -ōris, *m.,* numbness, paralysis

torqueō, -ēre, torsī, tortum, to twist, hurl

torrens, -entis, *m.,* torrent

torus, -ī, *m.,* couch, bed, marriage-bed

tot, *adj.,* so many

totidem, *adv.,* just as many, the same number

tōtus, -a, -um, *adj.,* total, whole, entire

trahō, -ere, traxī, tractum, to draw, drag

trāiciō, -ere, -ēcī, -iectum, to strike through, to throw across

tranquillus, -a, -um, *adj.,* calm, tranquil

trānseō, -īre, -iī, -itum, to go across, change

trānsmittō, -ere, -mīsī, -missum, to pass through, pierce

transtrum, -ī, *n.,* cross-beam, bench

trepidō (1), to fear, tremble, be in distress

tremō, -ere, tremuī, to tremble, quake

trepidus, -a, -um, *adj.,* trembling, fearful

trēs, tria, *adj.,* three

tristis, -e, *adj.,* sorrowful, grim, ghastly

triumphus, -ī, *m.,* triumph

tropaeum, -ī, *n.,* trophy

truncus, -ī, trunk

tū, *pron.,* you (s.)

tueor, -ērī, tūtus sum, to regard, consider, protect

tum, *adv.,* then, next

tumidus, -a, -um, *adj.,* swelling, swollen

tumultus, -ūs, *m.,* tumult, turmoil

tumulus, -ī, *m.,* burial mound, grave

tunc, *adv.,* then, at that time

turba, -ae, *f.,* crowd, multitude, mob

turbidus, -a, -um, *adj.,* stormy, turbulent, troubled, confused, in confusion

turbō (1), to disturb, disrupt

tūricremus, -a, -um, *adj.,* incense-burning

turriger, -a, -um, *adj.,* turreted, turret-crowned

tūs, tūris, *n.,* incense

tūtus, -a, -um, *adj.,* safe

tuus, -a, -um, *poss. pron.,* your (s.)

tyrannus, -ī, *m.,* tyrant

uacō (1), + *abl.* to be free *or* empty of, + *dat.* have time for

uacuus, -a, -um, *adj.,* empty, free

uadum, -ī, *n.,* shallow, ford

uaesānus, -a, -um, *adj.,* mad, crazed

ualidus, -a, -um, *adj.,* strong

uallis, -is, *f.,* valley

uallum, -ī, n., rampart

uastus, -a, -um, adj., vast, huge, massive

uātēs, -is, m. or f., prophet, bard, poet

ubi, adv., where, when

ubicumque, adv., wherever

ubīque, adv., everywhere

-ue, conj., or

uehō, -ere, uexī, uectum, to carry, convey

uēlāmen, -inis, n., robe, covering

uēlifer, -fera, -ferum, adj., sail-bearing

uēlum, -ī, n., sail

uēna, -ae, f., vein

uēnābulum, -ī, n., hunting-spear

uenerābilis, -e, adj., venerable, majestic

ueneror, uenerārī, uenerātus sum, to revere

ueniō, uenīre, uēnī, uentum, to come

uentus, -ī, m., wind

uēr, uēris, n., spring

uerber, -eris, n., blow, stroke, lash

uereor, uerērī, ueritus sum, to fear, respect

uergō, -ere, uersī, —, to turn, decline

uersō (1), to revolve, turn over

uertex, -icis, m., top, peak, head

uertō, uertere, uertī, uersum, to turn

uērus, -a, -um, adj., true, genuine

uerūtum, -ī, n., spear, javelin

Vestālis, -e, adj., of Vesta

uester, -tra, -trum, poss. pron., your (pl.)

uestrum. See uos

uestīgium, -ī, n., track, trace, footstep

uetō, -āre, -uī, -itum, to forbid, prevent

uetus, -eris, adj., old, former

uetustās, -ātis, f., age, antiquity

uia, -ae, f., way, path, road

uīcīnia, -ae, f., nearness, approach

uīcīnus, -a, -um, adj., neighboring, situated nearby, + dat.

(uicis) abl. uice, f., change, succession

uictor, -ōris, m., conqueror, victor; as adj., victorious

uictōria, -ae, f., victory

uictrix, -trīcis, f. adj., victorious, conquering

uideō, -ēre, uīdī, uīsum, to see

uideor, -ērī, uīsus, to seem

uīlis, -e, adj., cheap, worthless

uinco, -ere, uīcī, uictum, to conquer, defeat

uindex, -icis, m., defender, champion

uindicō (1), to claim the right

uiolō (1), to violate, profane, pollute

uiolentus, -a, -um, adj., violent

uir, -ī, m., man, husband, warrior

uīres, uīrium, f.pl., strength

uirtūs, -tūtis, f., bravery, courage, excellence, masculinity

uīs, *f., defective noun,* force, power

uiscera, -um, *n.pl.,* entrails, guts

uīsus, -ūs, *m.,* sight, gaze

uīta, -ae, *f.,* life

uītalis, -e, *adj.,* vital, of life

uīuō, -ere, uixī, uictum, to live

uix, *adv.,* scarcely, with difficulty, reluctantly

ullus, -a, -um, *adj.,* any

ultimus, -a, -um, *adj.,* furthest, last, final

ultrā, *adv.,* further, beyond

ultrix, -īcis, *adj.,* avenging

umbra, -ae, *f.,* shade, shadow; ghost

umquam, *adv.,* ever

uncus, -ī, *m.,* hook

unda, -ae, *f.,* wave

unde, *adv.,* whence, from where

unguis, -is, *m.,* nail, claw, talon

ūnicus, -a, -um, *adj.,* only, sole, single

ūnus, -a, -um, *adj.,* one

uocō (1), to call, summon

uolgātus, -a, -um. *See* **uulgātus**

uolgus. *See* **uulgus**

uolnus. *See* **uulnus**

uolō, uelle, uoluī, —, to want, wish, be willing

uolt = uult

uoltus. *See* **uultus**

uolucris, -is, *f.,* bird

uoluō, -ere, uoluī, uolūtum, to roll, revolve, turn over

uōs, *pron.,* you (pl.)

uōtum, -ī, *n.,* prayer, vow

uoueō, -ēre, uōuī, uōtum, to pledge, wish for

uox, uōcis, *f.,* voice, sound, word

urbs, urbis, *f.,* city

Vrbs, Vrbis, *f.,* Rome

urgueō, -ēre, ursī, —, to press upon, follow up

ūrō, -ere, ussī, ustum, to burn

usque, *adv.* right up to, continuously

ūsus, -ūs, *m.,* experience, use

ut, *conj.,* + *indic.,* as, when; + *subj.,* so that, with the result that

ūtilis, -e, *adj.,* useful, valuable

ūtor, ūtī, ūsus sum, + *abl.,* to use

uulgātus, -a, -um, *adj.,* common, ordinary

uulgus, -ī, *n.,* crowd, people, multitude, mob

uulnus, -neris *n.,* wound

uultus, -ūs, *m.,* face, expression, look

Xanthus, -ī, *m.,* the river Xanthus

Zmyrnaeus, -a, -um, *adj.,* of Smyrna